SAMS
Teach Yourself

Unix

Robert Shimonski

in **10** *Minutes*

800 East 96th Street, Indianapolis, Indiana, 46240 USA

Sams Teach Yourself Unix in 10 Minutes

Copyright © 2005 by Sams Publishing

International Standard Book Number: 0-672-32764-3

Library of Congress Catalog Card Number: 2004098030

Printed in the United States of America

First Printing: June 2005

08   07   06   05   4   3   2   1

Trademarks

All terms mentioned in this book that are known to be trademarks or service marks have been appropriately capitalized. Sams Publishing cannot attest to the accuracy of this information. Use of a term in this book should not be regarded as affecting the validity of any trademark or service mark.

Warning and Disclaimer

Every effort has been made to make this book as complete and as accurate as possible, but no warranty or fitness is implied. The information provided is on an "as is" basis. The author and the publisher shall have neither liability nor responsibility to any person or entity with respect to any loss or damages arising from the information contained in this book.

Bulk Sales

Sams Publishing offers excellent discounts on this book when ordered in quantity for bulk purchases or special sales. For more information, please contact

U.S. Corporate and Government Sales
1-800-382-3419
corpsales@pearsontechgroup.com

For sales outside of the U.S., please contact

International Sales
international@pearsoned.com

ACQUISITIONS EDITOR
Jenny Watson

DEVELOPMENT EDITOR
Scott Meyers

MANAGING EDITOR
Charlotte Clapp

PROJECT EDITOR
Mandie Frank

COPY EDITOR
Laura Town

INDEXER
Tim Wright

TECHNICAL EDITOR
Christopher Heinz

PUBLISHING COORDINATOR
Vanessa Evans

INTERIOR DESIGNER
Gary Adair

COVER DESIGNER
Aren Howell

PAGE LAYOUT
Brad Chinn

Contents at a Glance

Contents

Part II   Navigating the Unix File System

Part III   File System Utilities

Part VII   Tips and Tricks

Part VIII   Appendix

About the Author

Robert Shimonski is a well-known networking and security expert consulting out of the Long Island, New York area. Rob has authored over 30 books on information technology that include topics specializing in systems engineering with Unix and Microsoft technologies, as well as networking and security design with Check Point and Cisco technologies.

Rob has also deployed state-of-the-art technology in hundreds of companies worldwide—just recently designing and implementing a global MPLS network spanning hundreds of sites. Rob was fortunate to have been able to keep up with his love for Unix by deploying Linux systems and freeware networking and security tools such as Ethereal, NMIS, and MRTG, to name a few.

Because of Rob's unique blend of Unix- and Linux-related real world experience, Rob has served as a technical editor and author on countless Unix- and Linux- related articles and books. Rob was also the networking and security expert chosen to help develop and design *LinuxWorld Magazine*. You can view *LinuxWorld Magazine* at http://www.linuxworld.com. To learn more about Roberts's book projects, please visit him at www.rsnetworks.net.

Acknowledgments

I would like to thank everyone who helped me create this book—a personal thank you to all who went the extra mile when we needed it most. The editors, thank you very much for giving me the tools I needed to make this book a reality.

Jenny Watson, thank you for presenting me with this project and working with me to develop it. My technical editor, Christopher Heinz, and developmental editor, Scott Meyers, for working with me through "crunch time" and being my extra eyes on the printed page.

We Want to Hear from You!

As the reader of this book, *you* are our most important critic and commentator. We value your opinion and want to know what we're doing right, what we could do better, what areas you'd like to see us publish in, and any other words of wisdom you're willing to pass our way.

You can email or write me directly to let me know what you did or didn't like about this book—as well as what we can do to make our books stronger.

Please note that I cannot help you with technical problems related to the topic of this book, and that due to the high volume of mail I receive, I might not be able to reply to every message.

When you write, please be sure to include this book's title and author as well as your name and phone or email address. I will carefully review your comments and share them with the author and editors who worked on the book.

Email: opensource@samspublishing.com

Mail: Mark Taber
            Associate Publisher
            Sams Publishing
            800 East 96th Street
            Indianapolis, IN 46240 USA

Reader Services

For more information about this book or another Sams Publishing title, visit our website at www.samspublishing.com. Type the ISBN (excluding hyphens) or the title of a book in the Search field to find the page you're looking for.

Introduction

Welcome to *Sams Teach Yourself Unix in 10 Minutes*

Welcome to *Sams Teach Yourself Unix in 10 Minutes*. If you are new to Unix or just want to learn more about it, you have undoubtedly chosen the perfect companion for your journey. Whatever your reasons were for picking up this book, you will be glad that you did, because it is filled with useful information to help you learn Unix. This book's mission is to ensure that you walk away with a fundamental understanding of Unix, how to navigate and use it, and how to become more productive with it. Another goal of this book is to show you other avenues for gathering information that will help you continue your education beyond the lessons herein.

Unix Overview

Because of growing market share from companies such as Red Hat, Sun, IBM, and Novell, it's no wonder that Unix is becoming more and more of a household name. Unix (and Linux, which is Linus Torvald's version of Unix) is now found in most firewall and Web-server-based systems as well as all the way to the desktop for end user productivity and development. Unix has deep roots in the computer industry. First surfacing in universities and the military, it began to grow more and more in use with the massive development and expansion of the Internet. Once Linux was released, the landscape of Unix changed forever. Now, Linux (an easier to use version of the Unix operating system) and Unix are both found almost everywhere you look, and to ignore them is simply impossible.

Some common versions of Unix (called distributions, or distros for short) you may have heard of are Sun Solaris, IBM AIX, FreeBSD, Red Hat Linux, SuSE Linux (also known as Novell SUSE), and SCO ACE. Although these versions of the Unix operating system have differences, they all share the same thing: a basic Unix kernel that can be openly worked on and developed by anyone with the knowledge to do so. In this book, we will focus on the similarities between all versions of Unix so that you can use any one of them and still be productive.

Unix is a very powerful multitasking operating system. Multitasking refers to performing multiple tasks at once; in this context, it more specifically means that a user can run multiple programs simultaneously within one single logon of the system. Unix is also a multiuser operating system. What this means is that many users can simultaneously (and securely) use the same machine. In addition, Unix is open source software, which means that users are free to look at and modify its code. This is not the case with proprietary versions of Unix, but most versions are open source, so unless you are working with a specific vendor that does not allow its version of Unix to be altered, it's safe to assume that most versions (especially Linux versions) can be modified. Another powerful tool to unleash with Unix is the power of coding and scripting. Entire user communities work with and help develop Unix programs, and this is what keeps the system growing, developing, and getting better each and every year. This is not commonly seen with other proprietary operating system platform vendors such as Microsoft. Most of these vendors release closed source systems, which means you cannot freely write code that works blindly with these systems.

There is much more to learn about Unix. You are encouraged to find out more about its history and origins on the Web; this way, we can focus more written pages on teaching you how to use Unix. (At the end of this book, however, there is a reference section that will help you locate additional information on Unix, its history, and where it is going in the future.) So, now that you know that Unix is rapidly growing in use, let's take a second to understand why this book is so important, how this book should be used, how this book is organized, and how you will learn Unix productively.

Versions of Unix

Before we get too involved in this book, there is one thing that needs to be made clear: There are many versions of Unix, also called flavors or distros (short for distributions). In this book, all versions will be referenced as "Unix" unless there is something specific that needs to be said about a certain version or distribution. Since Unix, Linux, and all its cousins are so similar, they are said to be in the same family, but as you know, people in your family don't all look or act the same, do they? Nonetheless, you can think of Unix as a family of sorts, one with a great heritage, many grandparents, and plenty of recorded history to laugh about.

This book (just like the first edition) has been written to be as general as possible and to not favor any one vendor or implementation. This way, you can learn in the least confusing way possible; after all, the more complications you are exposed to while learning, the more your learning progress is hindered. Again, in this book, Unix is Unix unless otherwise noted.

 If something in an example doesn't work on your system, don't be alarmed—check the online manuals or ask other users of your machine. Different versions of Unix sometimes have slightly different versions of commands—it will be worth your time to learn how things work on your system as well as how things work on other distributions of Unix.

Teach Yourself Unix in 10 Minutes

In each 10-minute lesson, you are given a small amount of material to master. In most cases, the material in each lesson builds on that presented in the previous lesson, so although you can jump around between lessons, you will be best served to start the book at the beginning and move through it in order. You can come back and forth as you master each lesson, in case you forget a command or how to do something.

This book is divided into seven parts. Part I, "Learning the Unix Environment: Baby Steps," covers logging in to a Unix (or Linux) system so you can begin to learn Unix. You will learn how to get into Unix (and Linux) so that you can work within it. Part I also shows you the essentials of how to help yourself, which is important when using any new system.

Learning how to find and use documentation is one of the keys to survival when it comes to learning Unix. Part II, "Navigating the Unix File System," covers the file system, how to navigate it, and so on. Part III, "File System Utilities," explains how to manipulate and work with files as well as how to use some of the tools that come with the system to edit, archive, and compress files. Part IV, "Working with the Shell," covers working with the shell and how to use scripts. Although you won't become a master of shell scripting overnight, you will start to see how powerful Unix can be if you know how to work with it. Part V, "Environment Customization," covers user utilities as well as how to modify your environment. Part VI, "Networking and Communications," is new to the second edition of this book; you will learn how to print with Unix as well as how to set up basic networking and security. Part VII, "Tips and Tricks," covers advanced topics and some Linux so that you can work within Linux (since it's easier to get and use) and learn Unix in the convenience of your home or anywhere else you may want to put a new Linux- or Unix-based system.

How Do You Use Unix?

Unless you're simply using a Unix machine as a platform for a prepackaged commercial application, most of your interaction with Unix is likely to be textual commands typed at a command-line prompt. Most implementations of Unix do provide a graphical user interface (GUI); however, even when running the GUI, much of what you are likely to do involves typing commands into terminal windows that are available in the GUI. We will be covering both in this book, because some versions of Unix install graphically as well as allow you to initially log in to the system graphically. This being said, it is imperative to learn the fundamentals of both methods if you are to progress past the login portion of this book presented in Part I.

So, are you worried about minimal graphical help? You shouldn't be; that's why you are reading this book! As previously mentioned, you will learn both graphical and textual methods in this book. Dragging and dropping and using a mouse are still options in some Unix systems, but the strength of Unix is at the command line. You will see this as you read through each chapter. You will be introduced to K Desktop Environment

(KDE), one particular flavor of such an interface, in this book. KDE was chosen as a representative sample for this book because it is available on a wide range of Unix systems and distributions. KDE is also the default environment for SuSE, which is owned and operated by Novell, one of the best-run and supported versions of Linux available today.

 As tempting as it might seem, you are cautioned not to become entirely dependent on GUI utilities even if you have a GUI product with the sophistication and convenience of KDE. This book focuses on the command line, because the command line is where most of the power lies. The GUI is only something that has gradually been developed to get more users to work with Unix; it bridges the gap between drag-and-drop on Microsoft Windows and the Unix command line. Remembering that the true power lies in the command line is what is going to make you into a Unix expert. For example, there are some commands that you can't do or can't do completely from the GUI; that alone proves that you do lose power when you use the GUI. Try not to get too accustomed to using it, but feel free to use it to help you learn Unix.

Getting More Information

It is impossible to provide in-depth coverage of even a small fraction of Unix commands in a book this size. Instead, you are provided with enough information and knowledge to get you started, allow you to master the fundamentals, get you involved in the Unix system, and to get you to the point where if you need more information, resources, and answers, you will know exactly where to start looking for them. In fact, this book concludes with an appendix with a list of online resources in case you ever need to use them.

Who This Book Is For

This book is for anyone who wants to begin learning Unix or learn beyond the fundamentals. The book's small size is meant to keep your investment in time down to a minimum and to give you the greatest amount of knowledge possible based on the time you contribute to learning.

This book also serves as a handy quick reference to using very common commands, so even as you move beyond the basics, you can still use this book as a desktop reference. The commands presented in this book are universal and can be used on a great many Unix versions, so make sure you refer to this book in the future if you forget a command or how to do something.

Author Note

Before we begin, I would like to take a second to put your mind at ease. Unix is not simple; it never was, and it never has been. Having worked with Unix in a production environment for years on just about every different version, flavor, and distro, it is easy to see why so many folks hate working with Unix. It's not easy to learn, mostly because it's not intuitive at all. Unix is something that needs to be learned before it can be attempted. In a Windows operating system, being intuitive can get you places; in Unix, it usually will get you nowhere. You simply have to learn the basics from a book like this to be able to start to be productive. Although this isn't true for everyone, it applies to most people I have encountered. After teaching for years and writing a great many books about business and technology, I can easily see why Unix can be intimidating.

This book's goal is to destroy that intimidation; to give you a tool set to work with, and to send you on your way into the world of Unix with a foundation to grow on. So, let's begin to learn how to make Unix work for you, with you, and definitely *not* against you.

Conventions Used in This Book

This book uses the following conventions:

- Information you type appears in **bold `monospace`** type.

- Screen output is shown in `monospace`.

- Menus and menu options, keys you press, and names of buttons and other screen components with which you might interact appear in **bold type**.

- The **Return** key is synonymous with the **Enter** key.

In addition, this book uses the following sidebars to identify helpful information:

 Notes present you with special information that you need to be aware of.

 Tips lead you to shortcuts and solutions that can clear up confusion or save you time.

 Cautions help you avoid common pitfalls.

 Plain English explains new terms and definitions.

LESSON 1
Getting Started

The first lesson we will learn in this book is how to get started using Unix by connecting to and logging in to your Unix system with a set of credentials. We will also cover the concepts behind text-based and graphical-based logins, as well as how to log out.

Unix has been around for a long time; before Y2K and the growth and explosion of the Internet, Unix was used in systems everywhere. Throughout the years, instead of continuing to be known as a difficult and unfriendly system for new users to learn, Unix has grown into a multi-vendor supported, easy to install and use, documented desktop and server-based operating system, growing each day more powerful than anything ever dreamed of.

This was no overnight phenomenon, of course; Unix has expanded each year thanks to tons of ongoing open source developmental efforts, the continuing development of Linux, as well as the Unix install base growing exponentially yearly. Not only growing is the presence of Unix, but also so has its fan base, which includes users of Unix as well as Unix System Engineers. With this growth rate, more and more people (whether they like it or not) are using Unix at home and in the workplace; perhaps you are reading this book because you are one of them. In order to unleash the power of Unix, you must first understand its foundations. In this chapter, we will cover how to take the most basic steps in using Unix:

- How to log in to Unix both graphically and textually

- How to log out of Unix both graphically and textually

We will also discuss KDE, a graphical user interface (GUI)–based login. You will need to know how to connect to your system to properly utilize KDE. We will also cover all the concepts surrounding these steps, such as the differences between text-based and graphical-login, and security. An additional goal of this chapter is to expose you to other new concepts that you will expand on in later chapters.

Practicing with Unix: It Really Does Make You Perfect!

In this chapter we are going to learn to start using Unix, but before we do, a quick word about practice. It can't be said enough: Practice makes perfect. As with anything foreign to you, as long as you can read this book, follow along, and walk through the steps outlined, you will eventually develop the speed you see from an experienced Unix operator and feel comfortable using Unix.

When new learners see the speed with which experienced Unix users enter commands, they often panic and feel as if they will always be novices because they cannot recall commands as quickly as they would like. Do not think that you aren't knowledgeable because you can't type remembered commands quickly; as long as you know what you are doing, speed is not a factor. Start small and take baby steps, but practice to develop recall ability. To a new learner, Unix commands can look like a foreign language, and in a way, they are. Apply the same concept of how to learn a new language such as Spanish, English, or Chinese to learning Unix commands. Repetition builds your ability to recall. You will only be able to recall these commands and recall them quickly if you practice. When you get a copy of Unix, install it on your home PC and practice the commands; the commands will become familiar to you in no time. The more you practice the commands, the better you will remember them and the easier Unix will become. Of course, practice is not by any means mandatory for reading or completing this book. Getting a copy of Unix installed so you can practice and continue to expand your knowledge is completely up to you and for your own growth and benefit.

Another concept that is new to Unix learners is that even with the addition of graphical components to make the user experience much easier (such as the graphically based KDE), it's still imperative to remember that all the power of Unix is underneath the hood. You only have the ability to use all of what Unix has to offer if you use the command line. There are things that you cannot do from the GUI. Within the command prompt is where you will be most productive, but it is also where most people need help when it comes to Unix. Teaching you the fundamentals of unleashing the power of Unix from the command line is this book's primary mission. No fear, each step will be explained before we take it, while we are taking it, and after we take it. Many people don't understand how powerful and useful Unix can be until they know how to use it properly or are first exposed to the plethora of tools that come freely with it. Learning how to get shell access and run commands, this is essentially where we want to be, this is what we are going to work to get to, and this is what our ulti-mate goal is with this lesson. We want you to comfortably connect to a Unix system, and be comfortable in the Unix environment.

Prepare to Log In

Now that we have learned a little history and current presence of Unix, we should prepare to log in. Before we do, however, it's important to remem-ber the following: To log in to a Unix system, you will need to log in with credentials. Credentials are tied to accounts on the system and supplied by a system administrator. For example, with a Microsoft Windows desktop operating system such as Windows XP Professional, you would log in to the system with the Administrator account and use an assigned password configured by the administrator of that system to gain access. In Unix, the logistical setup for logging in is essentially the same. Other things to remember about the Unix login process are as follows:

- In Unix, there are different types of accounts. Some are more powerful than others, allowing you to do more or less depending on the rights and privileges assigned to them.

- The *root* account and generic user accounts are the most com-mon accounts seen on Unix systems. Root is the administrator's user account. It has the most privileges available to the system and can do the most harm as well. Putting too many privileges in the hands of users who do not need them can be dangerous and is strongly discouraged.

- Try to create individual user accounts so that each user can be tracked by security measures such as auditing and logging. These new accounts would have far fewer privileges and would be able to do far less than the root account. (On a related note, if you are using Unix at work and have such an account assigned to you, think about the ramifications of practicing at work without permission.) You can also control access to many user accounts at once by assigning users to groups. Generally related to security, groups are categories of users who have access to certain data or have a category of privileges specific to their assigned permissions.

- Unix is a multiuser platform. This allows for multiple users to log in to the system simultaneously, set up their own environments, and so on. Because Unix enables multiple users to access the system simultaneously, you can be working on a large calculation on a spreadsheet while another user on the system is running another type of calculation of some sort. Many different processes can run simultaneously on a single computer by hundreds of different users. Lesson 11, "Managing Processes in Unix," will continue to build on the concept of processes and how you can learn to use and manage them.

- Unix is case sensitive. Typing commands in Unix can be confusing to operators of Windows because Windows is forgiving with case sensitivity; for example, typing a command in the Windows command prompt in lowercase and in uppercase produces the same results.

Usernames are tied to accounts; the account name is usually the username used to log in, whereas the password is the challenge, or the response to trying to use that set of credentials. In other words, the password is the information you must enter to gain access to the system. It's a security measure used to prove that you are who you say you are; if you can supply the password, you are able to connect to your system and work within the environment configured for you by your administrator. A Unix system administrator is the person who would configure an account on the system for you, supply you with credentials, and get you started. Don't forget: Usernames and passwords are assigned to accounts on the system, and your credentials are your username and the password you use to access the system once prompted. Let's use these concepts now to begin our login process.

Prepare to Log In   Now that you know the gist of getting started with Unix, before you start the next section, take a look at your keyboard and ensure that your Caps Lock key is not selected. This will cause many mistakes with the login process if overlooked! Remember, Unix is case sensitive, and this is a common mistake that causes headaches for many new Unix users.

The Login Process

The first step is about to begin, so get yourself ready. You are either at the Unix console or you have remotely connected to your system using a terminal emulation application.

Terminal Emulation   One of the most common ways to connect to a Unix system is remotely. The reason why Unix systems are commonly remote to you is because they are usually kept protected and secure in a designated location. You can connect to them with a service called Telnet, which provides terminal emulation. This is covered in greater depth in Lesson 18, "Networking and Security."

As mentioned before, once you attach to the system, you will be asked for your credentials, which consist of your username and password. After you supply this information, Unix will continue by loading your user

environment. Your Unix system administrator will have already configured this for you, and he or she will have given you appropriate rights and
permissions to do what you need to do on the system. After you successfully log in, you will see a command prompt awaiting your command.
Now, before we continue, let's clarify something of extreme importance.
There are two ways to log in to Unix: either via text-based login, which
we will cover in the next section, or with a GUI, which will be covered
after we discuss text-based login. Even if you log in via a GUI, you can
still get to a shell prompt within the GUI. This will be explained later.
What is important to remember at this time is that our goal is to get to the
command line, even if you have to navigate a GUI-based login to get
there.

Text-Based Login

Text-based login takes us right to where we want to go: to the command
line or shell prompt.

Something that can be confusing to Unix learners is that text-based login
screens vary between Unix distributions (also commonly nicknamed
distros), and although login screens are becoming more similar, they are
still different enough to cause annoyance to most new users. Most text-
based Unix login prompts look like this:

```
login:
password:
```

When you see the login: prompt, type your username and press return.
The password: prompt appears immediately thereafter. When you have
successfully typed in both your username and password, you reach what
is called a shell prompt. This is the most common way you will see login
and password prompts, and any deviations will be simple to figure out.

When logging in to your system, it's important to remember a few things
that will most likely cause you frustration or stop you from logging in.
These include the following:

- Ensure that case sensitivity is not an issue when supplying your
  credentials.

- Make sure you are supplying the correct credentials.

- Make sure that if you have supplied the correct credentials, your account settings are not an issue. Your account could be configured so that if you try too many wrong passwords, you are barred from attempting to enter any new ones.

- Make sure that you do not backspace, because in some distros of Unix, you will find that backspacing does not work. Type carefully to save time.

After you have completed the login process, you will be ready to take the next step and proceed to the next lesson. Before we move on, though, let's learn about KDE and the GUI-based graphical login process.

 Secure Your Credentials When you are asked to enter your password, Unix is kind enough to block it out on your monitor from prying eyes. It does so to maintain security over the system so that your credentials do not fall into the hands of others who could impersonate you and cause damage to the system. Prying eyes can't see you type your password on the screen as you type it; they can watch what you are typing on your keyboard. This is a common practice, so be aware of it and keep your credentials safe. If you think that your credentials may have been compromised, ask your system administrator or help desk to change them immediately if you do not have authorization to change them yourself. Just like anything else in life, if you spend some time thinking of and considering security, the less likely you are to have a security issue.

Graphical Login

Throughout this first chapter you have heard about how to log in to Unix via text-based login. With KDE (which stands for K Desktop Environment), you have the option of graphically logging in to your system. Here, when your Unix system starts up, it goes through the same boot-up process until it gets to the login prompt. Instead of the text-based login screen, however, the X Window System environment launches. From this environment, the graphical environment or shell in which you will work is loaded. The most common graphical environment is KDE, although GNOME is also common; both are covered later in this chapter. To log in to Unix graphically, you will be presented with the same credential request, but instead of seeing it in the command line, you will see it in a dialog box. After you supply the correct credentials, you will be logged in to the system, and you can continue your work or lessons.

Consider a graphical login. Instead of sitting down at your Unix terminal, you may be sitting in front of your home PC with Linux installed. You boot up your system and are presented with a dialog box with the same basic information such as needing your credentials (username and password), but you may have other options available to you as well, such as the ability to change the session type. In any case, other than for the presence of a few commands that you can see graphically and manipulate with your mouse, text-based and graphical logins are still requesting the most basic of information, which is your username and password.

 Keyboard Shortcuts   When using Unix, you should get used to some new keyboard shortcuts because you will be working within the command line more and more. Knowing a few shortcuts can save you a lot of time when navigating the shell. Use the Tab key within the GUI to shift fields. For instance, after you type in your username, use the Tab key to get to the next field. This will allow your hands to remain on the keyboard and not have to reach for the mouse. This is one example of how you can save time while navigating not only Unix, but also the keyboard.

The Logout Process

You have completed working in your Unix session and now want to log out. Whether graphically or text-based, you should consider a few things before you do. Logging out is also a fairly simple process. There are a few important things to consider when logging out. First, before logging out, always remember that Unix is a multiuser platform that could be serving hundreds of clients at one time. Make sure that you consider these users as well. When you log in, you identify yourself to the system. Therefore, Unix knows about any files you open. Unix knows when you decide to log out; if you forget something such as a program you may have left running during the logout process, Unix will close it for you because it has tracked your activity. This is one example of the power of Unix.

Another concern is security. To remain logged in to Unix all the time is also a security risk. You should always remember to log out whenever you are done with a session. Here is one example of how forgetting to log out can hurt you. Imagine being at work and logging in to a system in the morning and leaving at the end of the day and you forget to log out. Consider that someone else could wander along and now change things in the system "as you," because he or she would be logged in with your credentials. Remember that credentials are your username and password, which usually tie to an account on the system with your personal information associated with it. Now, things were changed, you don't know what was changed, even if you say it wasn't you, it was your account. This could lead to significant problems, so better to be safe than sorry. In short, learn to log out and understand the importance of it.

Logging out of a Unix system is fairly easy. Let's take a look at how to do it using both text-based and graphical methods.

Text-Based Logout

When working within the shell prompt, all you need to do to log out is type "logout." The command would be seen as

```
>logout
```

Once you issue the logout command, the Unix system will immediately return to a login prompt. You have just successfully logged in and out of a Unix system. If it was your first time, you should be proud of yourself—this was quite an accomplishment. If you have done this once or twice before, continue to practice, because practice makes perfect and this is one task you will master in no time. Remember, you must log in to a Unix system to work within it. Also remember that even though this may have been a somewhat easy task, there were many things to consider, mainly your environment, your security, and your data integrity. One last thing to mention about logging out would be to consider the many different distributions of Unix available today. Some distros may not accept the logout command. Some expect other commands such as `exit`. A common error message of "Not login shell" may indicate the need for the `exit` command.

Graphical Logout

When logging out of your Unix system graphically, you will need to take more steps than when logging out using the text-based method. When logging out of a text-based session, you simply need to issue the command. Within a graphical environment, you need to manipulate the graphical environment itself to log out. The icon you see that indicates the main menu in which the logout process is initiated from may vary depending on your Unix distribution, but in most all cases, the first icon (sometimes represented as a K or the SuSE logo), which produces the `Logout…` command from menu. Once selected, you will be given an option to end your session, turn off your computer, restart your computer (warm start), or simply cancel your logout and go back to your current session.

A House with No Mouse   Don't forget your keyboard shortcuts such as the Tab key. Remember that not all systems come with a mouse, but all require a keyboard. This is determined by systems BIOS upon startup. You will always have a keyboard to work from, so you should really consider practicing logging in and out of your Unix system without the use of your mouse as much as possible. It's not common to find mice on Unix systems.

Shell Game

You are now the master of logging in to and out of Unix. If you are not a master yet, then continue to practice until you are; each lesson after this one builds in complexity, so this skill must be mastered to continue. As was previously mentioned, the true power of Unix is within the text-based environment, where you can execute every command completely. Again, the only problem with this is knowing how to manipulate these commands. Another thing to consider is what shell you are working within. Experienced Windows users will know that Windows, when conceptualized, was intended to run on top of DOS (disk operating system). Windows installed on top of DOS to make a complete operating system. Windows was the environment, and there were a few different versions of DOS available.

Now, apply the same concept to Unix. The shell (the shell prompt you just worked within to log in and log out) can also be changed. You applied KDE to get your environment. The concepts behind all shells are the same, so now that you understand what a shell is, let's go over the different types available and most commonly used.

 This Shell Smells a Bit Fishy   One of your goals while learning Unix should be to not let any of the lingo scare you. A shell is nothing more than a preference. Most commands and functionalities are the same between shells. Unless you are a hardcore developer and well versed in Unix, most times, you will use and continue to use whatever environment you grow accustomed to learning. However, one great thing about Unix is the fact that you can change your shell easily once you know how. This adds a deep layer of flexibility into an already powerful engine.

As we just mentioned, Unix has a wide variety of shells that you can choose from, and many of the major differences between them are related to programming with them. Programming is usually based around the need to try to automate a process or job. With this in mind, remember that the shell you select changes the way you program. To automate jobs, you can write a shell script. A script is nothing more than a file that calls commands to automate a process. We will learn more about shell scripting in Lesson 14, "Shell Scripting Fundamentals."

> **Shell Scripting Is Very Powerful**   A script is very similar to a DOS batch file. For those of you with Windows and DOS skills, comparing DOS batch files with Unix shell scripts is like comparing a piece of sand with the desert.

For those of you new to Unix, you will probably have to use whatever shell is available to you, unless you are able to install Unix and manipulate it yourself. In this section, we will explore only what shells are most commonly used and what their benefits are; your shell selection is your own choice and your own preference. In any case, the shells that are most commonly used today are as follows:

- **sh**—The Bourne shell: This is one of the most commonly seen shells, and it is available on just about any Unix distribution in use today. The Bourne shell offers a simple scripting syntax and is the most commonly used and learned by Unix users.

- **csh**—The C-shell: The csh shell takes its name from the C programming language. A programming language is similar to shell scripting in which it uses the same concepts of automation, but takes it to a high level. The scripting environment that is offered by csh is similar to the C language and offers enough flexibility to write lengthy, customized scripts that run on most Unix machines. Most developers will be familiar with csh.

- **tcsh**—The extended C-shell: If you are familiar with csh, then tcsh will be no mystery to you. Some of the shell extensions available with tcsh include filename completion and an accessible command history.

- **bash**—The Bourne-again shell: This is the default shell available on most Linux systems.

In Lesson 15, "User Utilities," you will learn to change to a different shell. If you can't select your shell and begin this book with the one you want, never fear: By the end of the book, you will be able to. For now, let's get comfortable with getting beyond the login and logout process and issuing commands to the shell prompt so we can be productive.

Working Within the Shell

As a Unix user, you will find yourself working within the shell almost all the time. As you do, you will undoubtedly run into common issues and problems. One of the common problems was mentioned before: While working within Unix, make sure your Caps Lock button is not selected, because Unix commands are case sensitive and will not function properly if entered in the wrong case. In some situations, you could select the wrong command by using improper capitalization. Another common problem is not having the command's location listed within the PATH environment variable (covered in Lesson 16, "Modifying Your Environment").

 Follow the Path   To easily understand the PATH environment variable in Unix, compare it to the PATH statement in Windows. By typing **PATH** at the Windows DOS or command prompt, you can see the same information. For example, if you want to run a calculator in Windows, typing **calc** at the command prompt will do it. This happens because calc.exe is located in one of the directories listed within that PATH statement. The layout of Unix is similar.

Another issue you may have to contend with at the command prompt is what appears to be a hung process, which in reality (if it isn't a hung process) is really nothing more than a program that has been started and left running and that appears to be unresponsive. An example of this can be seen in Figure 1.1.

- Here, I have run the vi editor, which is nothing more than a Unix-based word processor. The vi editor, once launched, seems to hang the Unix session for the user and gives the unknowledgeable user the feeling of being completely trapped. In this situation, some users who don't know how to fix this will power off the system and reboot. Others will try common Windows commands that will in fact work in some cases.

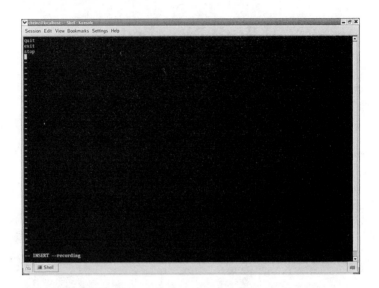

FIGURE 1.1 The terminal is unresponsive because a program is running in the foreground.

- To break out of the vi editor, I selected a series of keys that, when pressed in sequence, help stop the running program and return me to the normal shell prompt. The command sequence I used in this example was pressing the **Ctrl** key and holding it and then selecting the **z** key. This interrupted the program and returned me to the shell prompt. Some helpful commands are as follows:

  - **[Ctrl+d]**—This tells the computer that you are done sending input to a command. This is useful if you've accidentally started a program and can't get out.

  - **[Ctrl+c]**—This is the Unix break character. This usually kills any program that is currently running and returns you to a command prompt.

- **[Ctrl+z]**—This command suspends the process you are currently running and returns you to a command prompt. This is the keystroke sequence I used to break out of the vi editor in the previous example.

Now that you are more familiar with your current environment, let's recap what we've learned about shells. Shells are important, but if you know one, you can usually perform the same commands from shell to shell and have the same functionality with little variance. This book's content is based on the fact that you may not be able to select your shell, so most if not all of the content will apply to any Unix system you may be working with. Remember, as you become a more advanced user, shell selection will become more important.

Summary

You should now feel comfortable working within your environment. You can log in and log out, and you should understand the simple concepts surrounding the login and logout processes. You should also know how to run these processes in both a text-based and a graphical environment.

In Lesson 1, "Getting Started," you learned how to get started with Unix, but it does not stop here—it has only just begun. Before continuing, make sure you know how to log in and log out of your system as well as how to access the shell prompt and issue basic commands. In this chapter, you logged in, opened a program, shut it, and logged out. Now, armed with this knowledge, let's move to Lesson 2, "Getting Help." In Lesson 2, we dig into the built-in help system for Unix, a place where new users should go before quitting or admitting defeat. Believe it or not, the Unix help system is very helpful. Before we go on to Lesson 2, make sure you have mastered this lesson, because you will need to apply it to each subsequent lesson as we move forward in the text.

LESSON 2
Getting Help

In this lesson we will cover how to get help. Many times you will find yourself looking at a Unix console or computer screen and feeling a little clueless. This lesson will teach you how to handle those moments.

As more and more features are added to today's high-speed computer networks, these networks are becoming increasingly complex. In turn, as networks and systems evolve, develop, and become more complicated, additional help and knowledge are needed in many areas, especially when it comes to the infamously cryptic Unix. Some people would say that the sheer beauty of this situation is that few users know that Unix comes with its own built-in help system that, if used properly, can actually help teach you Unix. Now that you have learned to log in and connect to a Unix system, this chapter will focus on one of the most common things you will do as we progress through the rest of the book: getting help when needed. This chapter will not only cover how to use the built-in help system, but it will also make sure that you know other ways to help yourself in time of need.

Make no mistake, learning Unix is not impossible, and if you take the right steps to learn it, it can be grasped. The help system and other forms of assistance are there for you to use when you forget things or want to learn new commands or explore the system further. In this lesson, we will cover a number of ways that you can find help in Unix. These include using the man pages and other forms of Unix help as well as online resources and other resources you may be able to access as you learn Unix.

What's the Problem? This lesson talks about getting or finding help for Unix. It does not cover how to solve any technical problems you may have, which is usually a job for a help desk technician. This chapter revolves around how to get assistance when learning Unix, not how to fix it if it is broken, which is beyond the scope of this text.

Finding Help in Unix

It should come as absolutely no surprise that products such as Microsoft Windows have built-in help systems; perhaps you have even used them. Most common computer operating systems do have detailed help systems built right into them. Unix is no different, and although it seems to have been around as long if not longer than many other operating systems, it also has as detailed a help system as any.

Unix was created without a thought to being user friendly; it was built for power, functionality, flexibility, and control. Because Unix is generally a command-line-driven system, there is commonly no mouse to point and click; therefore, the help system is not easy to find if you don't explicitly look for it or don't know where to find it. However, the joke is on us: Once you know how to use the Unix help system, you need only go to a shell prompt and type the correct command to access it. You don't need to point and click unless you are navigating in an X Window System environment.

If you know how to access the built-in help system in Unix, it can help you perform just about any command known in the system. You should be aware, however, that each version of Unix has its own version or form of help, and these forms may not be identical. For instance, SuSE Linux and Red Hat Linux have commands that do not match. This does not mean that the commands are not similar or that they will not perform the same exact function. Sun Solaris–based Unix and FreeBSD have different commands as well, but most of the core functionality is the same. Although there may be differences in the names of commands, most commands are identical by design. If you can't get a command to work, it may just mean that you are typing in the incorrect syntax for your particular system. This is another example of why you should use the system's *manual pages*, or *man pages* for short. In cases such as this, the man pages are all you need to get the help you require.

Always remember, the power of Unix is found in the commands you use, so to have a way to constantly check whether something is wrong or whether the syntax for a specific command is correct is helpful, to say the least. Again, this can be done using the man pages.

Using the Unix Man Pages

Man pages are nothing more than compressed text files, located in /usr/share/doc. The information included is a command reference. Occasionally there are even known bug statements found within man pages. One thing is for certain, though—man pages are helpful if used properly.

As programs grew increasingly complex, they began to tax the man page format, so the info help format was created. These pages include a hierarchical structure, hypertext links for easy navigation between documents, and keyboard and mouse navigational tools. The first time you use info help (often when looking for help in the Emacs text editor), it can be a little overwhelming, but this format is not difficult to use once you have a feel for it.

Want to Know More?   To learn more about info help, type **info info** at the shell prompt. This will allow you to read the tutorial.

As we will learn in the following sections, there are also many resources on the Internet that include man pages. For example, man pages can be found on Google or the Linux Documentation Project.

As just mentioned, you will eventually need some form of help in your Unix journey. Not all of your issues will be addressed in the man pages, but many of them will be. Help comes in different forms. For example, you may need help with a command such as ls. The ls command is used to list the names of files that are found in your current directory. In the man pages, you may see the syntax on the use of ls but not necessarily understand what you need to do with it. In other words, your problems may run deeper than the help provided in a man page. This is where time, practice, reading, and learning save the day. The man pages are only for your reference; they will not do anything for you unless you are able to understand what they say and perform the appropriate actions.

So why use man pages instead of the Internet or any other resource? To answer this question, remember the purpose of the man page: It's there to help you, not to do the work for you. All the information you need for the command syntax is found within that man page. If you want to look for further suggestions on use, then that's a different story. But why look outside the box when you have the answer inside the box? Check the man page first before you move on to other resources.

In addition, there is no definitive source for Unix information on the Internet. There are scattered resources that can help you if you know the specific vendor of the product you are using (SuSE, AIX, SCO ACE, and so forth) and the vendor provides support documentation. You may also find some good information if you are a master at searching the Internet, but chances are that this information will be secondhand at best. Because Unix users have always relied upon the system's own internals for assistance, man pages are the best-known resource for you as a Unix student. These pages are anywhere Unix is unless the files or links to them are damaged and in need of repair. To review, benefits of man pages include the following:

- Man pages are the quickest and easiest source for complete information on how to use the commands on your system.

- Man pages provide information on what programs do and how to use them.

- Man pages cover other related utilities that you might be interested in working with. The recommendations on these pages could also be of help to you.

- If you're a programmer or developer, man pages will also provide helpful programming information that you can use when coding and writing scripts.

To display a manual page, use the man command. By simply typing **man** followed by the command you want to look up, you will get the results you need.

```
>man ls

NAME
       ls - list directory contents
SYNOPSIS
       ls [OPTION]... [FILE]...
DESCRIPTION
       List information about the FILEs (the current directory
by default).
(...)

(output removed)
```

In this example, the man pages showed you all the available syntax you can use with the ls command. You can use this information to get added details on the command.

As you can see, man pages do not enter a command for you, and they don't help you do a task—they are simply informative. When using man pages, what you are looking for is additional information about a command; that way, you can customize the command with the many different switches that can be applied to it.

As you use man pages, you may find them unwieldy and long. Never fear, because there are shortcuts to using the help system. These are in the form of apropos and whatis.

Commands You Need to Know   When you see a . . . on your screen, there's more text to be read. What you need to do is press the **Spacebar** to see the additional text.

The man pages won't scroll automatically, so you may need to carry out this extra step. To stop this action, press **q** to quit the page and return to the command line.

More Help

Now that you are familiar with the built-in help in Unix and how to use the man pages and the man command, we will look at some other ways to use man. We'll also explore the use of apropos and whatis, two programs that can help you find additional assistance.

As mentioned earlier, the man command can often generate unwieldy results. This can be especially problematic if you just want to see a subset of the information on a man page. If this subset is all you need (for example, if you only want to view a summary description of a command), then you can use the following commands:

```
whatis
man -f
apropos
man -k
```

Using any of these followed by the command you are interested in (just like the man ls example) will result in a shorter set of information being supplied back to you. Let's look at each of these commands in detail.

whatis and man -f

The man command used with the -f switch is similar to the whatis command, just as apropos is similar to the man command with the -k switch. The full power of most Unix commands can only be unleashed with the use of switches, so make sure you pay close attention to how they are used in this lesson and in the rest of the book.

Switches and Flags As just mentioned, you can find help simply by using switches with the man command. That's great to know, but what exactly is a switch?

A switch (also called a flag) is used with a command. The command will perform the basic task, but the switch (when added) will modify the command. For example, in the last section, we covered the man command. Now, we are discussing man -k. The -k is the switch. Similarly, in the man -f example, -f is the switch.

You must remember that Unix is case sensitive. Uppercase and lowercase switches mean different things, so use them carefully.

By using man -f or whatis followed by a command name, you will get a description summary of that command. For example, to print a description summary for the date command, type the following, and a short description of what date does will be returned. Press **q** to return to the command line.

```
>man -f date
date (1)            - print or set the system date and time
END
```

There should be a whatis database on your system. If it has been removed from your system or never created, you may get an error reported back to you. Ask your Unix system administrator for help, because privileged access to the Unix system is needed to create a database if one does not already exist.

apropos and man -k

When using the apropos or man -k commands, you will see similar functionality to the whatis and man -f commands, but what makes these commands different is that they can help you find a result based on a possible match. In other words, if you are clueless about what command you want help on but have some idea about it, entering that idea with apropos or man -k will return a result if any partial matches can be made.

Try running apropos on time and compare your results with the results from the similar whatis time command:

```
>apropos time
clock (3)           - Determine processor time
clock (n)           - Obtain and manipulate time
convdate (1)        - convert time/date strings and numbers
date (1)            - print or set the system date and time
difftime (3)        - calculate time difference
ftime (3)           - return date and time
ftpshut (8)         - close down the ftp servers at a given
                      time
kbdrate (8)         - reset the keyboard repeat rate and
                      delay time
ldconfig (8)        - determine run-time link bindings
metamail (1)        - infrastructure for mailcap-based
                      multimedia mail handling
nanosleep (2)       - pause execution for a specified time
nwfstime (1)        - Display / Set a NetWare server's date
                      and time
parsedate (3)       - convert time and date string to number
...
```

In this example, we see quite a few results displayed, but we also see the ..., which means that there are even more results that are not shown onscreen. Sometimes, if you are not sure what you are looking for and are too vague in your request, you can get hundreds of responses. Searching through these results is time consuming, so use apropos and man -k as a last resort for finding help if needed.

Even More Help!

Just when you thought you couldn't find any more help, there is
more…there is even a built-in help system for specific commands. Why
would you use this if you already know how to use the man pages? Well,
the man pages aren't as easy to use as the built-in help system because
they take more time to load and aren't as quick to reference. For many
Unix-based commands if you need to find help, - -help provides the
information you need. In some cases, it might even be as simple as just
typing -h, or -?. Remember, Unix distributions can have small differences, and you may be able to abbreviate in one distribution whereas in
another, you may not. In addition, this method may not work if the help
system is damaged or unavailable.

To view the built-in help for the date command, type the following:

```
>date --help
Usage: date [OPTION]... [+FORMAT]
  or:  date [OPTION] [MMDDhhmm[[CC]YY][.ss]]
Display the current time in the given FORMAT, or set the
system date.
```

-d, --date=STRING	display time described by STRING, not 'now'
-f, --file=DATEFILE	like --date once for each line of DATEFILE
-r, --reference=FILE	display the last modification time of FILE
-R, --rfc-822	output RFC-822 compliant date string
-s, --set=STRING	set time described by STRING
-u, --utc, --universal	print or set Coordinated Universal Time
--help	display this help and exit
--version	output version information and exit

...

This information is much easier to read and utilize, but it does not contain
the depth of information that the man pages contain.

Graphical Help (Using KDE)

SuSE is one of few software companies that still provide printed manuals that try to help users once they move beyond installing the product. Buying the boxed version of SuSE Linux Professional gives you two thick books: the *Administration Guide* and the *User Guide*, which can both also be found online. These books have a fairly easy-to-read style that will have you using the product in short order. These books can also help you learn Unix/Linux.

The SuSE Help Center (covered in the following section) is basically a copy of the same documentation built within the system and found by simply clicking an icon on your desktop.

Searching the Help Center

Open the Help Center by typing `susehelp` from the shell, or click the lIfe-preserver icon in either the KDE or GNOME. Both will open the Help Center for you to peruse.

Once in the Help Center, take a look around to see whether the help there resembles the help you would expect to see in the man pages. You will find that both the graphical and text-based versions of help are useful in assisting you to work with and learn Unix.

Additional Documentation

When using Unix in the workplace, you should have a system administrator who is in charge of the Unix system and who may operate it. This staff member should already have documentation set up for the Unix system he or she cares for. This includes disaster recovery and security logs and other forms of documentation, such as maps or logs.

Another handy source of information that many systems administrators have exists in the form of a handbook that is usually given to new users on the network. Ask whether one exists for the Unix system you are working on. This handbook may provide you with another source of information that you can learn with and utilize.

When working with Unix at home, you may want to keep this book and several Web links available for more information if needed.

 Do Your Documentation! Documentation is extremely important. It is critical to know how your systems are designed and interconnected, what operating system (OS) they use, and so on. This may not be your area of expertise or experience, so it's important to have these things written down and to update them when necessary.

There are also other forms of documentation that you may encounter on a local intranet or on the Internet, where online information can be found and used quickly. The next section takes a look at a few of these resources.

Unix and Linux Resources Online

Unix resources can be found online quickly if you use a search engine to locate them. Using your favorite Web browser, run a search for "unix help" or "unix commands." You can even be more specific. The results should keep you busy for quite some time. In addition, some of the most helpful Unix- and Linux-based sites on the Web as of the printing of this publication include the following:

- **http://www.unix.org/link_list.html**—This is a massive list of links that will help you find more information if needed.

- **http://www.suse.com/**—This is the English-language home of SuSE Linux. News, downloads, and support are all available.

- **http://www.tldp.org/**—The Linux Documentation Project home page is a great place to go for general Linux questions and to learn about many of the applications included in your SuSE Linux distribution.

- **http://glue.linuxgazette.com/**—This is the home page of GLUE, or Groups of Linux Users Everywhere. Use this site to find your nearest Linux Users Group (LUG).

- **http://linuxgazette.net/**—The goal of the *Linux Gazette* is "making Linux just a little more fun." This electronic magazine is oriented toward new Linux users. Send your question to The Answer Guy.

- **http://www.google.com/linux**—This link takes you to the Linux-specific Google search page.

- **http://www.x.org**—This is the home page of X.org, the hub of X Window System development activity.

- **http://www.kde.org**—This is the online home of the K Desktop Environment. It's a well-organized site with links to nearly everything relevant to KDE.

- **http://dot.kde.org**—The KDE News site has links to online articles about KDE and its applications and also connects you to press releases and the like.

Appendix A, "Learn More About Unix: Reference" also lists more references and helpful links.

Summary

There are many help resources available for Unix. Depending on your needs, you can approach your search for information in several ways. The following are some methods with which you are now familiar:

- **Unix Manual Pages**—Use the man command to display full information about a specific command. The apropos, man -k, man -f, and whatis commands can display summary information and search for a specific type of command.

- **Built-in Help System**—Many programs have built-in help that can be displayed with a command-line argument, usually --help or -h.

- **Documentation**—Every installation of Unix ends up with a little something that reflects the personality of the system administrator, so every installation is a little different. Local documentation can help you find your way around the places where your installation differs from the collective norm.

- **Online Resources**—The Linux Documentation Project provides an excellent starting point when wading through the mountains of Linux information online. Remember, even though the information is specifically for Linux, most of it applies to other Unix variations as well. The `comp.unix.*` newsgroups are also extremely useful for hard-to-find answers.

- **The Graphical KDE Help System**—KDE provides excellent built-in help for most of its applications. Simply select Contents from the Help menu that is located in each application.

LESSON 3

Interfacing with Unix Graphically

In this lesson you will learn the fundamentals of the X Window System, a graphical desktop environment used to make working in Unix even easier.

Overview of the X Window System

Being able to log in to Unix and get help is a great start. You now know how to access a Unix system, but once you are in it, then what? Well, if you are sitting at a console or computer, you may just see a cursor waiting for you to type something. You may, however, be in a graphical user interface environment, also commonly known as a GUI. We touched on this in earlier lessons, but now we are going to get deeper into the concept and the X Window System.

What's Under the Hood? When considering what the X Window System is compared to the shell, consider this: The X Window System is actually run on top of the command-line interface you are starting to learn, and it helps you point and click your way around Unix instead of having to do everything at the shell prompt. Using the GUI actually limits you because of this. The GUI is not able to use all the power of Unix, because only at the shell prompt can you unleash all of Unix's internal power.

How Many Windows Are There?

The X Window System comes in both proprietary and open source forms. There is a great deal of development in this area, and as more development happens, the better (and easier) working with Unix will become. But don't fear—the current versions of the X Window System happen to be very good and fairly user friendly if you are already familiar with some form of GUI, such as Microsoft Windows.

The X Window System is simply referred to as X. There are also revisions of X, so you will commonly find a number following the X when you see it. Here is an example of the current version of X:

```
X11R6.8.2
```

Right now, X is at X11, or its 11th major revision. What about the R6? What does that mean? Well, that's easy to explain. The R and the 6 (also known as Rn) indicate the minor revision level. Together, X11 and R6 show current progress as the application develops and grows. In sum, it's just *cooler* (and easier) to call it X.

X Window System Functionality

The X Window System, when deployed, functions as a server. Just so you know what that is, a server application (which differs from what you may be currently using as a "client") runs and provides resources for other programs and system functions.

 In a Class by Itself   The X Window System is an application that will provide a set of interface display functions. Other environments such as Microsoft Windows and Apple Macintosh do not.

When a client wants to make use of the X Window System display and change settings, the client will make a request to the server to make such changes.

Client/Server—Same Computer With the X Window System functioning as a server, it does not matter if the client and server are not on the same computer; they can be running separately as well as running over a computer network.

There is a lot to learn about X, and because there are so many versions, it's hard to cover all of them in one lesson. Because of this, your homework assignment is to follow this lesson as closely as you can, and after you complete it, if you want to learn more about your version of the X Window System, search www.google.com/linux and www.x.org for additional information.

Starting the X Window System

We're now ready to start X! Let's begin. Starting the X Window System is easy. To start X, you only need to type commands at the shell prompt. First, make sure you are at the shell prompt, logged in and ready to go. You may already be in the X Window System; if this is the case, close out of it and reopen it to get the experience of loading it. Please note: If you are doing this at work and unsure of what you are doing, you may want to first ask for permission from your system administrator or whoever handles the administration of your system.

If you booted up your system and it went directly into X, this means that the system has been configured to do so automatically. If it didn't, you can configure it to load automatically if you like.

To start the X Window System manually after you log in, type the following:

```
>startx
```

There are two primary ways to load X: either a shell script called `startx` (which is also known as `x11` in some distributions) or the `xinit` program. Using `startx` will automate function calls to `xinit`, and thus is the preferred method to start X. In Lesson 14, "Shell Scripting Fundamentals," we will cover shell scripting in more depth.

Now that you know how to start the X Window System, let's talk more about it and what you need to know about starting applications.

After the X server starts itself, you will need to start some X applications as well. There is a default set available upon boot-up. A file called .xinitrc is located in your home directory. When Unix boots up, .xinitrc is automatically executed. Although this file is common, not all versions of Unix use it. Here are some examples of files used in other versions:

- Linux distributions use ****.m4 files.

- IRIX will use a secondary proprietary means if .xinitrc does not load initially.

The .xinitrc File Goes by Other Names   Just like many other things in Unix, there are variations in the name of the .xinitrc file in different distributions. Other known versions of this file include .Xinit, .xinit, .Xinitrc, or .xsession.

Remember, Unix is case sensitive, so having upper- and lowercase letters in your commands or switches can change the meaning of the command.

So what does an .xinitrc file look like? Here's an example:

```
#!/bin/sh
xrdb -load $HOME/.X11defaults
xscreensaver -timeout 10 &
xterm -geometry 80x30+10+10 &
```

An .xinitrc file, when dissected line by line, appears as follows:

- Line 1 states to use the Bourne shell, sh.

- Line 2 states to load the server resource database from the file .X11defaults in your home directory.

- Line 3 states to start the command xscreensaver, assign a 10-minute timeout, and then place the process in the background.

- Line 4 states to start an xterm (terminal), which is 80 characters wide by 30 characters high, placing it 10 pixels from the top and left of your screen.

The server resource database is discussed later in this lesson.

 What's with the Ampersand? For all programs you run out of the .xinitrc file (except your controlling process), end the line with an ampersand (&). An ampersand will make sure that the program you specify is run in the background.

Now that you understand the basics of the X Window System, the xinit program, startx, and the .xinitrc file, let's tie it all together so it makes sense and so you can learn how to make configuration changes to your Unix environment. This way, you can become more comfortable while working in your Unix environment.

Tying It All Together

The xinit program is used to start the X Window System server. The first client program listed will be launched. This is launched from /etc/init. In cases in which a program is not listed, xinit will look for a file in the user's home directory. This file (shell script) is called .xinitrc. If this shell script does not exist, you can create one in your home directory that can be used.

Let's look at this file again:

```
#!/bin/sh
xrdb -load $HOME/.X11defaults
xscreensaver -timeout 10 &
xterm -geometry 80x30+10+10 &
```

The first line in the .xinitrc file is used to declare the shell in which the script is written. Whatever shell you ultimately decide to use will dictate the commands you use within it. What this means is that if you use the C shell to write your script, you should be sure to use commands that are known within the C shell syntax.

In the first line of our example script, we see sh, which stands for the Bourne shell. sh is the standard Unix system command interpreter and will work for now if you use simple scripts. More complex scripting will require the use of a more complex shell, such as the C shell. sh executes commands that are either specified in a file or executed from the terminal where you sit.

In the next line of the example, you will see a personal initialization file called $HOME/.X11defaults. .X11defaults is nothing more than a profile file; that's it. You can edit your $HOME/. profile file by hand. We will learn how to do this in Part III, "File System Utilities," where we will discuss editing files in Unix.

Want to BASH Your Head into a Wall?   BASH is probably the most common Unix-based shell in use. Thanks to the worldwide use of Linux, BASH users have grown to countless numbers. Most like to use BASH instead of sh because there are no history features and no aliases in sh, which can become annoying. History is important when you do not want to retype the same command 100 times a day. With BASH, simply press the up arrow on your keyboard to recall commands already used and stored in your system's memory. If you press the up arrow and all that is reported back is gibberish and unreadable commands, you may be using an older shell.

Your next step is to launch any applications you may want to use. When viewing the example .xinitrc file again, you can see that programs such as an xterm window and xscreensaver are both launched in the back-ground. Think about what other programs you may want to start during the boot-up of your system. Helpful suggestions for what you may want to eventually add include a window manager and perhaps your e-mail client. No matter what you decide, the important thing to understand and learn here is how and where to make this change; once you know how to edit files, you can find things you want to launch and add them later.

In our example, the controlling process is the xterm window. When you close something that is designated as a *controlling process*, doing so will close you out of your entire X Window System session.

Let's look at another sample .xinitrc script:

```
#! /bin/sh
xrdb $HOME/.Xprofile
xsetroot -solid gray & xclock -g 60x50-0+0 -bw 0 &
xterm -g 60X24+0+0 &
xterm -g 60x24+0-0
```

You can see that this script is similar to the last one, and that is good. You will start to remember things such as this, and that's all it takes to learn Unix! In this sample script, you can see the power of Unix starting to open up; you can basically script anything and have it run automatically. You can even have scripts that call up other scripts—the flexibility is endless.

To continue with our example and tie this all together, let's examine the last line of the script. The last line should be your controlling process, and when you have a controlling process, this is the one time that you do not add the ampersand.

So what does this sample .xinitrc file do? With this file, xinit will start, and your .Xprofile file will be read. Once read, your environment will start to develop. In this example, the root window will be set to solid gray. A clock will be used. Two xterm sessions (one as a controlling process) and an xconsole window will be initialized.

Start xconsole Starting an xconsole window is always recommended. This is primarily so console messages do not appear on your screen. If you don't start an xconsole, you will have to keep refreshing your screen, which can be frustrating.

Window Placement

Now that you have started your Unix system and your environment has been initialized, you may want to specify specific window placement. You saw this in our original sample .xinitrc script:

```
#!/bin/sh
xrdb -load $HOME/.X11defaults
xscreensaver -timeout 10 &
xterm -geometry 80x30+10+10 &
```

You can set your window placement with the -geometry (-g) switch. Using -geometry is not difficult, as you can see from our example. Don't let the numbers scare you—they are nothing but settings. Once you know the command, the switch, and the settings, you can take a program like xterm and specify the size and placement of any window. The geometry of a window consists of its dimensions and its position on the screen. In our example, the geometry is specified by the numbers 80×30+10+10. These numbers can be easily broken down as follows:

- 80×30 is the window's dimensions. These numbers "size" the window.

- The position of the window is set by +10+10. This is not a math problem looking for a sum; it's the actual screen coordinates where the window will be placed.

This means that an xterm window with the dimensions of 80×30 will be launched at the screen coordinates of +10+10.

The .xinitrc script specifies this change from the default window size and location that are built into the program. If you do not like the placement of your window, go to your home directory, edit the .xinitrc file, and change the geometry to your liking. Once you boot up again (or startx), you will see your changes.

The xwininfo command can also be used to view sample geometry if you prefer to navigate the X Window System GUI. In Figure 3.1, you can see an example of this.

![Screenshot of a terminal window titled "cheinz@localhost:~ - Shell - Konsole" showing the output of the xwininfo command]

```
[cheinz@localhost ~]$ xwininfo

xwininfo: Please select the window about which you
          would like information by clicking the
          mouse in that window.

xwininfo: Window id: 0x1c00007 "cheinz@localhost:~ - Shell - Konsole"

  Absolute upper-left X:  4
  Absolute upper-left Y:  21
  Relative upper-left X:  0
  Relative upper-left Y:  0
  Width: 1016
  Height: 715
  Depth: 24
  Visual Class: TrueColor
  Border width: 0
  Class: InputOutput
  Colormap: 0x20 (installed)
  Bit Gravity State: NorthWestGravity
  Window Gravity State: NorthWestGravity
  Backing Store State: NotUseful
  Save Under State: no
  Map State: IsViewable
  Override Redirect State: no
  Corners:  +4+21  -4+21  -4-32  +4-32
  -geometry 1016x715+0+0

[cheinz@localhost ~]$
```

FIGURE 3.1   Using the xwininfo command.

Restart   To start the X Window System using your customized .xinitrc script, type **xinit** at your workstation prompt. If you receive an error when attempting this command, you may need to remove a lock file in your temp (tmp) directory. You can use the remove directory command (rm), which, when used with the appropriate switch and the appropriate path, will remove any problem files. Use rm -f /tmp/*, which will attempt to remove everything from your temp directory, or specify the actual file, such as by typing rm -f /tmp/.X0-lock.

We have taken a pretty deep look at the X Window System and how to customize it. Now, after learning how to log in, get help, and tweak your environment, you should start to gain comfort in working with Unix. In addition, although we have only worked through Part I, "Learning the Unix Environment: Baby Steps," of this text, you should feel comfortable running a few commands, and you should understand basic navigation if you are operating within a GUI. Let's move on to more customization and tips to help you work within Unix even more comfortably.

X Window System Look and Feel

It can only get better from here. Let's continue our lesson and learn more about customization. Launching the X Window System is mostly the responsibility of the particular window manager you've chosen to run. This section will help you learn which window manager to use based on your particular needs. For now, though, let's talk generally about what window managers can do for you and why you may want to use them.

Today, there are many window managers to choose from. Selection is good; it maintains competition, which leads to increased value in the products you use. As with all competing products, some window managers are good and some aren't. Although there are differences from one manager to another, all window managers are similar in operation. For example, most window managers for X are designed for use with a three-button mouse. The buttons on the mouse serve the following purposes:

- The left button is used for pointing, clicking, and selection.

- The center button is used for general functions, such as moving or resizing windows.

- The right button is used for application-specific functions, such as opening in-application pop-up menus.

You do not have to use this mouse layout and it can be changed. However, it's helpful to remember these designations if you want to implement and use the third mouse button for your Unix system, or if you want to know what all three buttons will do by default.

The X Window System environment also uses the concept of focused input when you type on your keyboard. What this means is that when you work with Unix, you can basically focus your input wherever you want as long as your system is configured to do so. In X, there are multiple options for focusing your input. Most window managers can be configured to

• Focus input on the foremost window

• Focus input on a selected window

• Focus input on whichever window the cursor is over

When you configure Unix to focus on the selected window, X does not need to be the selected window. It's also helpful to know that when you configure a window manager to focus input on whichever window the cursor is over, you can direct the input into a window that may be partially hidden. In Microsoft Windows and Apple Macintosh, the active window is the dialog box that is in the foreground. If you want to use a background application, you have to select it, thus bringing it to the foreground. With Unix, by simply dragging the mouse pointer over a background window, you can activate it and ensure that it's running as if it is in the foreground. Thus, as a learner of Unix, you may get confused and not be working in the window you thought you were. Be careful as you navigate and pay attention to where your mouse pointer is if you attempt to work in a window that does not appear active.

Let's review the .xinitrc file once more. When looking at the file, pay close attention to the xrdb command on the second line. What is this used for?

```
#!/bin/sh
xrdb -load $HOME/.X11defaults
```

To answer this question, we need to become familiar with the resource database, which is where the X Window System gets its configuration settings. Most configurations of X are handled by a server-based resource database. A client will make a request of the server. The server will check its database for the requested information. If the server has the information, it will provide it; if not, it will let the client know it doesn't have the information. It's that simple.

The server will check for user preferences based on the client that is requesting them. The command xrdb is what is used to load the database. Once X is loaded, xrdb is loaded immediately following. xrdb will also load the needed configuration from a *dot file*. Dot files will be discussed in Lesson 16, "Modifying Your Environment."

Check Your Documentation   Each version of Unix can be customized, and you may be working on an already-customized version. It takes a while to be able to modify your environment properly; many times, it requires trial and error or lots of reading. Reading the documentation stored locally on your system for whatever window manager you are using is a great start. Also, if you can set up a test Unix system to practice on, that is ideal. You can become a master of modification when you have a practice lab to work in.

In this section of the lesson, we have completed our discussion on customizing your X Window System environment. You should feel comfortable with the ways that Unix will attempt to set your environment when you load it, either by giving you a default .xinitrc script group of settings or by using a modified group of settings that you have created. Remember, we will learn more about how to alter files in the next few lessons, so you can come back to this section when you learn how to use vi or the emacs editors to make any changes you would like. Let's move on to a discussion of some of the window managers available today.

Window Managers

Window managers take over where the X Window System leaves off. X was made to be limited, and it can only go so far. When you want to get more advanced, you need something that will allow you to do just that, and that something is a window manager.

As a new learner of Unix, you may get confused when using a window manager. Unix is so customizable (again, a positive feature, not a negative one) that even if you are sitting next to a peer or friend who is using the same version or distribution of Unix as you are, you may see things completely differently on your screen based on how you have your window manager configured. Don't let this stress you—the best way to overcome this issue is by simply working within the environment and learning how to customize it yourself. As you do, your fear of the unknown will diminish rapidly.

There are many different window managers. In this section of the lesson, we will cover the ones you will encounter most frequently, including the most commonly used window manager: twm.

Using twm

twm is by far the most common and easiest-to–use window manager. It's not the most feature-rich window manager, but because it's commonly used by default, it has become the unofficial standard. When used properly, twm can provide you with an extensive experience beyond what you are accustomed to. There are many things you can do with this window manager, such as creating buttons to be used in windows, adding pop-up menus, and so on. To start twm, you only need to type the following at the shell prompt:

```
>twm
```

The window manager will then open if one is not already opened and conflicting with it. If you already have a window manager open, you may be denied from opening two of them at the same time.

 Where Are the Changes Stored? The file used to save all of the configuration changes we have discussed (as well as a plethora of others) is named .twmrc and is most likely located in your home directory.

Once you launch twm, you will be able to work within it to customize whatever it is you want to adjust. Make sure you read your local documentation, though, because there are many other window managers available, including the ones we will discuss in the next section.

More Window Managers

Unfortunately, choice often leads to complexity. Not only is this the case with technology in general, but it is especially true in the world of Unix and window managers. Because so many different window managers are available, we can't cover them all in granular detail. We can, however, take a quick look at some of the more popular window managers so that you will understand any major issues that may pop up when using them.

It is up to you to choose which window manager suits your tastes and needs. Once you have an idea of which manager you need and some experience using it, it will become increasingly easy for you to work in that manager in the future. Besides twm, other common window managers include the following:

- **AfterStep**—This window manager will add extra features such as graphical enhancement and fading abilities. To use this manager, you will need to have a good video card to prevent taxing your colormap.

 Colormaps   A colormap is really nothing more than a set of color cells assigned with manageable index values. In other words, a colormap consists of a set of entries defining color values.

- **ctwm**—This window manager is a tab-style manager with a 3-D animated look.

- **fvwm**—This is a popular 3-D virtual window manager. It is also the lowest in memory consumption and fastest in speed.

- **fvwm2**—This is the 2nd version of fvwm. It's different from its predecessor with more features for an even faster and easier experience.

- **tvtwm**—This is a version of **twm** that offers additional benefits such as virtual desktop capability.

- **Blackbox**—This window manager is common among users who don't like running the other larger window managers.

Remember, this is not by any means a complete list, and **twm** is the window manager most commonly used.

Now that you know what a window manager is and you are familiar with some of the different kinds of window managers you can deploy, you can grow into whichever environment suits your needs the best. Let's wrap up this lesson about the GUI with a discussion about using KDE, which stands for the K Desktop Environment.

Desktop Environments

In the past, Unix-based window managers have been used to manage the user's screen and apply customization. With the launch and continued development of Linux, this is changing at a rapid rate. The advanced desktop environments that come with Linux and newer versions of Unix now provide users with a more sophisticated experience.

There are many tasks you can do on the desktop, such as access most if not all of your programs, start a shell, and type in commands. You can also manage files, which we will start to cover in the next lesson, "The File System Explained." Although there are many other tasks you can carry out, these are the most common ones performed on any system.

 Ease of Use Can Be Career Limiting   Remember, the power of Unix is at the shell prompt. Do not get too accustomed to working with the GUI until you have mastered some of the aspects of the command line. Try to balance your learning using both methods; do not become dependent on the GUI.

KDE

In our final section of this lesson, we will cover KDE, which stands for the K Desktop Environment. There are many other environments you can use, with one of the most popular being GNOME. Another popular environment is the Novell Linux Desktop (NLD), which is similar to GNOME and KDE. You can see this environment by going to Novell's website at http://www.novell.com/products/desktop/.

Although many more environments are under development, KDE is still the most common, and because there is a lot of documentation on it, it is easier to learn. (Remember, documentation and research are important to learning Unix.) The growth of use in KDE is similar to that with window managers; thus, although there are many environments, use the one that best fits your needs. Remember, however, that KDE installs as the default shell in many popular Linux distributions, such as Novell's SuSE Linux Professional.

KDE is an excellent window manager and once mastered, it will allow you to do most anything. For example, KDE will allow you to customize your environment in whatever way you want or need. If you want to change your shell or modify your environment further, you will learn more doing so in Lesson 16, "Modifying Your Environment."

 Choose Wisely! Sitting on top of most copies of X these days is the K Desktop Environment (KDE) or the GNU Network Object Model Environment (GNOME). Choose whichever one best fits your needs. The only way to understand which one is right for you is to first define your needs and then research each desktop environment to see which one will serve you best. Install and utilize the environment that you want when you are ready.

So, how does KDE work with the X Window System? When you normally log in to SuSE, you use a graphical login screen, which we learned about in Lesson 1, "Getting Started." That screen is your first taste of the X Window System. Once you log in, your environment is configured. So, what if you want to change it? With SuSE Linux, you can use a tool called SaX (or SaX2). SaX2 is the X configuration tool for Novell's SuSE Linux. It runs for the first time during the initial SuSE Linux Professional installation, where it identifies your graphics card, installs the graphics drivers, and sets up X to its default configuration. These settings are conveniently stored in the .XF86Config file found in /etc/X11/XF86Config.

In addition to user interface sophistication, KDE provides an integrated suite of tools for configuring your machine. If you are a Windows or Macintosh user, then KDE will seem like second nature to you. It has the same point-and-click feel that other GUI-based operating systems like Windows and Macintosh also have.

If you're looking for a way to make your Unix experience feel a bit more like using your personal computer, then use KDE, but remember that the true power of Unix is in the commands you use at the shell prompt.

Summary

This lesson taught you about the background of graphical user interfaces in general and the X Window System in particular. The use of xinit and other system programs and utilities was also discussed. This lesson also covered how to customize your user environment. It ended with a discussion of window managers and desktop environments such as KDE.

- The X Window System is based on a client/server model.

- The xinit program is used to start the X Window System server.

- The startx shell script is used to initialize an X session, perform basic display functions, and so on.

- The startx command streamlines the process by combining commands into a file that can be referenced quickly.

- If a startup script filename is not given at the command line with the -x option, then the startx command searches for a file specified by the user's .xinitrc environment variable.

- In cases in which a program is not listed, xinit will look for a file in the user's home directory. This file is .xinitrc or whatever is specified.

- The file called .xinitrc will call other programs to load with basic settings that can be defined within the script, such as running in the background with the use of an ampersand (&).

- Client programs are launched from /etc/init.

- If .xinitrc does not exist, you can create it and add it to your home directory.

- The X Window System requires a window manager if you want to add niceties and conveniences such as title bars.

LESSON 4

The File System Explained

In this lesson, we will cover the fundamentals of the Unix file system as well as start to learn how to perform basic file system navigation.

Now that we have learned how to log in, find help, and navigate the X Window System, we need to learn about the single most important thing in Unix—the file system! Because almost everything in Unix is viewed as a file, it would only make sense that understanding the file system be your top priority. By the end of this lesson, you will know how to navigate the file system with ease. Unix provides extremely sophisticated file access and control, which is a clear sign of its internal power. Let's begin learning how to unleash that power.

File System Design

Unix's file system is one of the strongest and most flexible in use today. This file system was made for power and not for ease of use, so navigating it can seem somewhat cryptic. Try not to worry, however, because the purpose of this lesson is to help eliminate any potential confusion. In this section of the lesson, we will take our first step toward that goal by looking at some of the design features that make up the Unix file system.

In Unix, the file system is laid out so that there is a single root directory. This is unlike Microsoft Windows, for example, where Windows will have multiple drive letters such as C:\, D:\, and so on. From the single root directory in the Unix file system, the file tree sprouts. A sample file system tree can be seen in Figure 4.1.

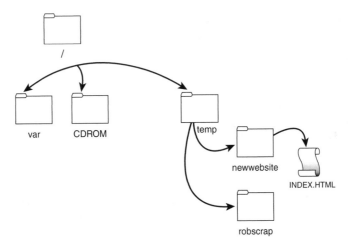

Figure 4.1   Sample Unix file system tree.

The root directory should not be confused with the all-powerful administrator account called "root," which we learned about when we learned
how to log in to Unix in Lesson 1, "Getting Started."

 Get to the Root of the Problem, but Which Root?
Remember, in Unix, the person with absolute control
over everything having to do with the machine is the
root user. The root user should not be confused with
the root directory, which is the one specific directory
on the machine that is considered to be the base
of the file system. Try not to confuse these two
definitions.

Another interesting fact about Unix's file system design is that installed
hard disks do not show up as drives in Unix. In Windows they do, but in
Unix, installed hard disks are viewed as directories within the file system.
In some people's opinion, this is easier to understand than the Windows
method. Here, if you have a drive installed on your system, you can

quickly change from your current location to this other drive just by entering the correct command at the shell prompt. Unix completely removes the end user's concern regarding what hardware is installed on the system and the physical location of the files he or she wants to access. One of the benefits of this design is that if you have a disk failure (where a hard drive ceases to function), then you are back in business as quickly as the disk can be replaced and remounted (this is a task for your Unix system administrator). Another benefit to this design is that you can quickly and easily find what you need in the file system right at the shell prompt, which we will shortly learn to do.

Unix commands, as we already discussed, are case sensitive, so the principle for searching for files is the same as that for executing them: You have to be specific.

Don't Be So Sensitive When learning Unix, always consider case sensitivity, no matter whether you are entering a command or searching for data. So many new users of Unix are accustomed to Windows and other operating systems that are generally not dependent on case sensitivity because they were built for ease of use. Unix, the powerhouse among operating systems, must be approached a different way.

Another aspect of Unix's file system design is its approach to file attributes. For those of you familiar with Microsoft Windows, attributes are characteristics assigned to files or folders that provide you some form of access control over the data. For instance, if you have a file that you don't want anyone to alter, you can make the file "read only." This ensures that if other people look at the file, they can't change it. In much the same way as Windows files, Unix files use three such attributes:

- Read
- Write
- Execute

In Unix, these three attributes can all be used in the negative form as well. In other words, you can make a file readable or unreadable, writable or not writable, executable or not executable. In most cases, files used for data will be designated as readable and writeable, and programs will be marked as readable and executable. This, however, is not a rule—it is simply what you are most likely to see in the types of files you are working with right now.

There's one last tip you should keep in mind when working in the Unix file system: You have to be careful when asking Unix to do something. Although you shouldn't be afraid of Unix, you have to consider that it does not have as many "checks" built into it as other operating systems. For example, if you try to change or delete something when working in Microsoft Windows, the operating system double checks with you to make certain that this is really what you want to do. This is not going to happen when you are typing commands into the Unix shell prompt. Thus, if you are practicing on a live system, be careful. Again, it's always recommended that you get a copy of Unix or Linux and practice in a lab so that you can make mistakes and not have to worry about them negatively affecting the system.

So, now that you feel comfortable with the design of the Unix file system, let's take a look at how to navigate it and at what commands you can use to unleash Unix's power.

Navigating the File System

File system navigation is commonly one of the first lessons taught in Unix, not only because of the reasons that were just discussed, but simply because it helps to know where you are and where you are going in order to get to your destination. It's like planning a trip—you don't just walk out, hop in the car, and go; there should be some planning involved, especially based on the complexity of the trip you are about to take. In Unix, knowing what commands to use is your preparation and plan, and once mastered, it will have you working on data files, editing web pages, and so on.

The most basic commands for dealing with the Unix file system are the ones for moving between directories and finding out what files are in them.

Using the pwd Command

For users of Windows or MS-DOS, one command you would commonly type at a command prompt is dir. This command (which stands for directory) will list the contents of the directory you are currently in; if you specify the entire path statement to another directory, the command will also let you see the contents of that directory. In Unix, the pwd (*present working directory*) command asks your machine to tell you what directory you're currently in. The way that Unix displays this information is different than in Windows. For example, in Windows, the path C:\Windows\Temp tells you that there is a folder (directory) called Temp in a folder called Windows, and the Windows folder is currently on the C:\ drive of the operating system. In Unix, the path will seem different; for instance, /priv/home/rob/temp/ would be an example of a path in Unix. Here, the simplest explanation of a path is that it describes the shortest set of directories through which you must travel to get to the current file or directory from the root directory.

Any time you're at the shell prompt, type **pwd** and Unix will tell you where you are as you progress in your Unix studies. The following is an example of this command at work:

```
> pwd
/priv/home/rob/temp/
```

Get familiar with this layout; you will be using path statements more and more as you progress in your Unix studies.

The Home Directory

In this book we have talked about the home directory a few times but have not yet fully discussed it. In this section we will now cover the importance of the home directory for the Unix user.

Each user in a Unix system should have one directory assigned to her for her personal use, to store data. This directory is called the *home directory*.

Your home directory will be where you wind up when you initially log in to your Unix system. You will be in your home directory by default.

Anything in or below your home directory belongs to you, and unless you allow otherwise, the contents of this directory will be secure and not available to others for use or browsing.

What Is That Tilde?   In Unix, you can refer to your home directory simply as ~. This is important to know because it can reduce the amount of typing you have to do. More specifically, to switch to your home directory, you can enter the tilde. When you want to switch to someone else's home directory, you can also use the tilde with the person's username, seen as *~username*.

Now that you can use the pwd command to find your present location, let's investigate how to view the contents of a directory, whether it be more directories or files.

Unix File Listing

Up to now, all the commands you have learned have been important. Not one of them is uncommonly used or seen. This next command we discuss, however, will be a command that you use just about all the time as a typical Unix user, so we will spend some quality time reviewing its details as closely as possible. The command you do this with is the ls command, which lists files. Issued without any arguments (also known as switches), ls lists the files and subdirectories in the current directory. You can, of course, list files in a different directory by specifying that directory in the path statement or simply by changing into that directory and then issuing the ls command. An example of using pwd and ls is seen here:

```
> pwd
/priv/home/rob/temp/newwebsite/
> ls
cgi_bin                    index.html
images                     vrml
```

This example is based on the assumption that I switched into the new directory I made (newwebsite) before issuing the pwd command. Then, by issuing the ls command, I got the file listing for that directory, which includes a new HTML page I created called index.html. Now, you try it. Attempt to determine where you currently are by checking your present working directory, and then list the files and other directories from your current location. As we progress we will learn how to change directories, but for now, master these two commands before moving on. Also, remember that this lesson is directed toward the Unix learner. If you know where you are in the Unix operating system, you don't need to issue the pwd command before listing files.

As mentioned earlier, if you are interested in listing files that are in another directory and you don't yet know how to change into that directory, then you can easily solve this problem using the ls *<directory name>* command. You can use the root directory we just learned about as your example. Because your current directory should still be your home directory, you can list the files and directories in root by doing the following:

```
> ls /
CDROM                      lib
bin                        priv
core                       tmp
dev                        temp
etc                        usr
include                    var
```

In this example, I have verified that all the data listed in the root directory are directories. This information may or may not be common knowledge, so if you are unsure, verify it with a command!

Use the ls command with the "long" option to ask Unix for more information in the listing. By issuing the command **ls -l *<directory name>***, you can view our example of the root directory in a whole different light:

```
> ls -l /
total 12
dr-xr-xr-x    2 root        512 Jan  8  1996  CDROM
lrwxrwxr-x    1 root          6 Dec  7  1995  bin ->
/usr/bin
-r--r--r--    1 root    7401946 Dec 24 20:15  core
drwxr-xr-x    3 root      11264 Nov  7 13:02  dev
drwxr-xr-x   11 root       3072 Nov  7 13:01  etc
drwxr-xr-x   46 root       2560 Jan 11  1995  include
drwxr-xr-x   23 root       4096 Oct 13 16:29  lib
drwxr-xr-x    4 root        512 Jul  4  1997  priv
drwxrwxrwx    3 root        512 Nov 24 00:30  tmp
drwxrwxrwx    3 root        512 Nov 24 00:30  temp
drwxr-xr-x   29 root       1024 Oct 27 17:53  usr
lrwxrwxr-x    1 root          8 May 21  1995  var ->
/usr/var
```

 Who Owns This File?   One of the cool things about the Unix file system design is that when you use the ls command, you can also see who the file owner is, which is an important piece of information.

As we discussed earlier in this book, it may be a little confusing to learn Unix if you have a distribution that is different than the norm. If this is the case, you may enter the ls command and get output that looks different from what you see here. That is okay. Different versions of Unix have ls commands that produce slightly different output. This does not mean that you will not be able to decipher it. Simply use the man command with ls to see what syntax is used and what you may be able to glean from issuing the command on your system. You can attempt to use the help command at the shell prompt as well. For the most part, you will likely see the exact same information each time, no matter what version of Unix you use.

Now that we have gone over how to see where you are and how to see what is in a directory, we should spend a moment learning how to read the output from the ls command a little better. Knowing how to do this will become increasingly important as you progress in your Unix studies beyond the beginner level. Consider the following example:

```
> ls -l /
total 12
dr-xr-xr-x    2 root         512 Jan  8  1996  CDROM
lrwxrwxr-x    1 root           6 Dec  7  1995  bin ->
/usr/bin
-r--r--r--    1 root     7401946 Dec 24 20:15  core
drwxr-xr-x    3 root       11264 Nov  7 13:02  dev
drwxr-xr-x   11 root        3072 Nov  7 13:01  etc
drwxr-xr-x   46 root        2560 Jan 11  1995  include
drwxr-xr-x   23 root        4096 Oct 13 16:29  lib
drwxr-xr-x    4 root         512 Jul  4  1997  priv
drwxrwxrwx    3 root         512 Nov 24 00:30  tmp
drwxrwxrwx    3 root         512 Nov 24 00:30  temp
drwxr-xr-x   29 root        1024 Oct 27 17:53  usr
lrwxrwxr-x    1 root           8 May 21  1995  var ->
/usr/var
```

Building Bridges   In this lesson and throughout the rest of the book, we will work at continuing to tie in the commands you learned in past lessons; this way, you can stay refreshed and see how to use commands together. Tying commands together is necessary in order for you to ultimately master Unix.

When studying Unix, think of your approach in terms of building bridges, because when you use commands, each one can build on another or be used with another to create more functionality. Unix commands were meant to be used in this way. In fact, the power of Unix isn't truly unleashed until you script a multitude of commands together to create a process or function.

In this example, which uses the ls command with the -l switch, you see what is located within the specified directory. Within that listing, you see the following details:

- The first line of output specifies the amount of content to be listed. In this example, the first line indicates that a total of 12 lines will follow.

- Each line after that is then listed with a subset of important information. Figure 4.2 breaks down each individual section of one line for you. The listing (here broken down into five areas) is actually incredibly easy to understand once you know what you are reading.

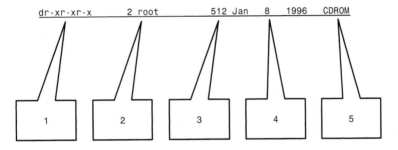

Figure 4.2 A sample Unix file system listing.

- Moving from left to right, section 1 of Figure 4.2 details the attributes of the data. As you'll recall, read, write, and execute are all attributes used to set access control on the data stored on your Unix system.

- A more granular breakdown shows r (read) and x (execute). There is also a letter d starting the line, which simply means that this line is specifying a directory, not a file. Lines that start with a - are for normal files, and lines that start with l indicate the directories known as bin and var. The l stands for link. Links will be covered later in this lesson.

- In addition, the attributes themselves indicate specific things that will be covered in greater depth in Lesson 19, "Configuring Permissions in Unix," where we take a closer look at file ownership and groups.

- In section 2 of Figure 4.2, you see the word "root." This simply indicates the user account that owns the specific data in this line listing. As you can see, root owns everything in the root directory. (Again, remember the difference between the two roots.)

- Section 3 of Figure 4.2 shows the amount (in bytes) of disk space that the data is occupying at this time.

- Section 4 of Figure 4.2 specifies the date of the last modification to this file or directory. January 1996 was the last time that this directory was altered in any way. Most times, unless you are using a data file such as the web page mentioned in an earlier example, you won't be making many changes to default system files, directories, or programs.

- In section 5 of Figure 4.2, we see the final piece of information: the filename itself.

In the next section, we will tie up our discussion of the ls command by learning about hidden data that you may be missing.

Hidden Data

You may be familiar with working with hidden data in Microsoft Windows environments. Unix is similar in that it too will also hide data from you. You need to be aware of this and also know how to view hidden data if requested or needed. What should alert you to the fact that things are hidden in Unix? Well, the file system will tell you about this data, as seen in the following output from the ls command:

```
> ls /
total 10
```

If you do the ls command and see you have a total of 12 lines but only 10 are viewable at the shell prompt, you probably need to add an argument or switch to the ls command, as seen in the preceding example.

We already learned about the long listing; now let us investigate those files whose names begin with a . (seen as a simple dot). These files are not shown by default, and the user must request to see them at the shell prompt. In this case, they can be viewed by using the `all` option for `ls`. The command would thus be seen as follows:

```
> ls -all /
total 12
```

You can see the difference in the two examples; one shows all twelve files, and the other shows ten files and hides the other two.

Now that you are comfortable using the `ls` command, you should know that Unix has many options for expanding on the `ls` command in addition to the ones discussed here. For example, options for sorting, for tabulating data, and for adding flags to a "short" listing to show a file's attributes can also all be used with the `ls` command. Beyond the `-l` and `-a` options discussed previously, some other options that you are likely to come across include the following:

- The `-F` option: This option is used to indicate file attributes.

- The `-R` option: This option is used to recursively list all files below a specified directory.

 Don't Forget Case Sensitivity   When using arguments such as the ones just listed, you will need to take note of whether they are in uppercase or lowercase. Remember that performing the wrong command in Unix can be damaging because there are few checks implemented to keep you safe from yourself. Make sure you use the help system if you are unsure about what switches you need to define to achieve specific actions.

That wasn't so bad, was it? Now, you can log in to Unix, get help if needed, perform basic navigation, see where you are when logging into Unix for the first time, and see what contents are contained within items in your path. If this is your first time doing these things and you were successful, you should be proud of how far you have gotten in such a short time period. After only a few lessons, you are now able to work within the Unix environment to some degree. In the next section, we will make even greater progress by learning how to begin "moving" around in Unix to find what you need or to do certain tasks.

Changing Directories: cd

Changing directories in Unix is just as easy as listing them. While the ls command is used to list the contents of a directory, the cd command is used to change directories. Moving from one directory to another may be necessary if you need to edit a file, delete a file, or perform any variety of tasks. The cd command will also help you exercise your use of other commands and allow you to better navigate the Unix file system.

Using the Unix cd command will let you change directories in a flash, but how do you know where you are and where you want to go? That's where the other commands you have already learned come into play. The pwd command will show you the directory in which you are presently located. The ls command used with specific arguments (if needed) will then show you the contents of that directory, perhaps files and other directories. If, in that list of contents, you see another directory you would like to access, you can simply use the cd command to do so. The full syntax for the cd command is cd <directory name>.

Because we've already learned about the home directory and the root directory, let's practice all these commands and move from one to the other and back again.

```
> pwd
/priv/home/rob
> cd /
> pwd
/
```

In this example, I knew where the root directory was located by default, so I just specified it. To move back, you can do the following.

```
> pwd
/
> cd /priv/home/rob
> pwd
/priv/home/rob
```

Notice that I didn't have to step back from the /rob directory to the /home directory and then from /priv switch and change directories to the root directory (/). I could simply specify /priv/home/rob when using the cd command.

Unix Commands Are Similar to Windows Commands...Sometimes The cd command used with Unix is identical to the one used with Microsoft Windows-based desktops when using the command or MS-DOS prompt. You can see this command and other Windows commands that are similar to Unix commands by going to start => run (or all programs => run) and typing **cmd** or command. Then, type the word **help**. The cd command (and many others) can be seen here. The cd command is common in use and structure in both systems.

Changing Directories: pushd and popd

After you master the cd command, you need to learn to move around Unix using the pushd and popd commands. pushd <*directoryname*> will need to be entered if you want to specify the directory. With the popd command, however, you will not need to specify a directory name.

When changing between directories, these two commands allow you to make good use of the directory stack. The *directory stack* is a type of data storage that works as follows: Data is added to the top, thus creating the stack, and the most recently added "plate" of data is the first to be removed if requested, because it comes off the top of the stack. To describe this in terms of the pushd and popd commands, data is pushed (pushd) onto the stack and popped (popd) off the stack when requested by each command, thus making use of these commands quicker and more efficient than use of the cd command. The following examples will show you how to perform both pushd and popd:

```
> pwd
/
> cd /priv/home/rob
```

```
> pwd
/priv/home/rob
```

Or

```
> pwd
/priv/home/rob
> pushd /var/adm
/var/adm /priv/home/rob
> pwd
/var/adm
```

Then

```
> popd
/priv/home/rob
> pwd
/priv/home/rob
```

Try both commands and see which is easier and makes more sense for you. Either one will work just fine with your distribution of Unix.

You now know almost everything about navigating Unix and its supposedly cryptic file system. Let's expand this knowledge by taking a deeper look at paths, which were briefly discussed earlier in the lesson.

Relative and Absolute Paths

When changing directories, you can specify exactly where you want to go by specifying the correct path. As mentioned earlier in the lesson, a path is the shortest set of directories through which you must travel from the root directory to get to the current file or directory. Unix, however, has two different types of path statements that you absolutely need to be familiar with in order to completely understand how to navigate the system.

The two types of path statements in Unix are relative path statements and absolute path statements. Paths starting with the root directory and ending in a file or directory name are called absolute paths. In other words, absolute paths have absolutely everything contained within them, including the root statement /. One example of an absolute path statement is as follows:

```
> cd /usr/local/bin
```

On the other hand, a relative path is a shortened version of an absolute path. It contains only the directory in which you are currently working, and it does not include the root statement /. Consider the following example:

```
> cd bin
```

Remember, relative paths are relative to the current directory. Furthermore, absolute paths start with / and relative paths don't.

By this point, you know how to find out where you are, what files are in what directories, and how to move to different directories. In this lesson, we have covered not only several important commands, but some important theory as well. Now that we have dug deep into using the shell prompt to navigate the file system, let's take a moment to learn how to do it with a GUI, namely, KDE.

Navigating the File System with the GUI

In this section, we will look at navigating the file system with KDE. KDE's file management system mirrors the shell prompt except that you are seeing a graphical representation of the same data that allows you to point and click with your mouse. Also, KDE's file management system is based on the web browser installed on the system. In this case, let's say that Konqueror is our web browser. To use Konqueror to navigate the file system, simply open the browser and use the location field to specify your path exactly as you would specify it at the Unix command line. If you so choose, you can also simply point and click your way wherever you want to go.

Also note that you can view websites at any time while working within Konqueror.

Simple KDE Actions

In KDE, files are represented with icons that usually indicate the file type. You can see an example of this in Figure 4.3.

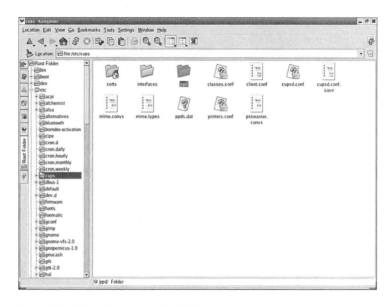

FIGURE 4.3   The file system in KDE.

As illustrated in Figure 4.3 directories are shown as folders, just as they are in Microsoft Windows. Double-clicking a directory is similar to using the cd command to get to that directory from the command line, but by navigating with KDE, you can access all your files and not have to type in a single command at the shell prompt. In addition, if you need to move or copy files, you can do so with the mouse by clicking on the file, holding it, and dragging it from Konqueror to your desired location. To delete files, simply drag the files you want to erase to the **Trash** icon. Right-click this icon and choose **Empty Trash Bin** from the context menu to complete the action.

In KDE, you can also use the following steps to create a new folder:

1. Right-click in the location where you want the folder to appear.

2. Choose **New** from the pop-up contextual menu.

3. Select **Folder** from its submenu.

If you need to get to your home directory in KDE, just look for the folder icon with a house on it. Clicking this icon opens a KDE file manager window showing your home directory. You can also attempt to navigate Konqueror by putting a tilde in the location field (remember the ~ is the same as your home directory, only shortened for your convenience).

If you spend a few minutes playing around with KDE, you'll find that its simplicity and elegance are on par with commercial desktop operating systems. You will also see that navigating files and directories either in the GUI or with shell prompt commands is not that difficult.

Summary

This lesson has given you the basic skills to work within the Unix file system. If you have any problems with this material, please practice it before moving to the next lesson. The following is a review of some of this lesson's specifics:

- Unix is case sensitive. Pay careful attention to case, especially if you're transferring files between a Unix machine and a personal computer.

- Unix files have three attributes: read, write, and execute. You can use these attributes to control access to a file.

- The pwd command tells you where you are.

- The ls command tells you what files are in a directory.

- The cd command takes you to different locations based on where you want to go.

- The pushd command remembers where you were, and the popd command takes you back to that location.

- Use relative paths whenever you can because they are shorter and easier to remember than absolute paths. It's usually much more convenient to use a relative path from your current directory than to use an absolute path from /.

- Remember that all these features and commands work together. Unix is about combining many small programs and features into a convenient tool that performs precisely as you want it to.

- Desktop environments can make your life easier; they automate many routine day-to-day tasks and provide a friendly face for some of the more difficult ones. If your system doesn't have KDE, don't fret—chances are that KDE can be installed on your system or that your system already comes with a nice desktop environment with comparable capabilities.

Lesson 5

File System Navigation Techniques

In this lesson you will use Unix to find files both at the shell prompt and with KDE.

Now that we have learned to navigate the Unix file system by changing directories and being able to list their contents, we need to learn how to search within the entire Unix file system for data based on our own queries. Imagine having to hunt for individual files that you think may be on your system. For example, what if you had an old spreadsheet on your system that you now need to use? Having created it five years ago, you can't recall where you saved it, but you remember a portion of its name. This is where using Unix's built-in help system comes into play.

In this lesson we will cover how to use the internal power of Unix to quickly locate data instead of having to manually search for it. When you are in a situation in which you know the name of a file but do not know where the file is, commands such as `grep` and `find` can help you gather the required information. Rather than using the `cd` and `ls` commands to search through the entire file system for data that may be located on your system, you can use other Unix commands that will help you locate that data. You can then go to that directory and list its contents. Let's start our discussion with the `find` command.

Using the `find` Command

When you need to find a file on your Unix system, you will need to know exactly where it is located (and navigate to it directly), or you may have to run a search on it because you aren't entirely sure what you are looking for. In either case, to locate a file on your system, you will need to know something about the file.

To find a file by its name, you will need to know a portion of the name. The more of the name you give, the quicker the search will be because that will narrow down the results. You can use wildcards to specify unknown characters. This same functionality can be seen in just about any other operating system, especially in Microsoft Windows. You can specify more than one file with a path by using wildcards. A wildcard is a character that matches many characters. The * wildcard matches any number of characters. A Wildcard will be explained more thoroughly and used in other (and more detailed) examples throughout the book.

If you do not know the name or part of the name, you will need to know something else about the file. Things that can be used as searchable criteria include creation date and the size of the file. The find command can then be used to build up matches to the query you construct and execute to find the data you need. In the next exercise we will learn how to use the find command.

To search for a file by name:

1. Before you search for a file, you have to have an idea of what you want to search for; therefore, specify the filename or some of its searchable criteria. Remember, you can include wildcards in the search for the filename.

2. Next, select the directory you want to search. If you want to search the entire file system, the starting directory will be /.

3. This command would appear as find <starting directory> -name <filename> -print, or if you wanted to find a specific file in the root directory, it would appear as follows:

```
>find / -name *.rpm -print
/var/lib/YasST2/you/mnt/i386/update/9.2/deltas/kernel-source-
2.6.8-24_24.13.i586.delta.rpm
```

Find Files...Now What? If you ask Unix to search for a file and do not tell it to print the results, Unix may find your file and tell you nothing about it. In most distributions of Unix, you will have to specify -print.

In this example, we searched the root directory for RPM files. RPM files can be used for installations and updates on your Unix or Linux system. This search method can be handy if you are unsure where to look for something you may need, or you want to save time by running a search to find files instead of hunting and pecking for them yourself.

Handling Error Messages   As you continue your search through the Unix system for files, you may encounter small problems, such as not finding your file at all, or you may get a message stating a problem or issue you need to be aware of. In this example, we see that there is an issue with finding the CD-ROM and floppy medium.

```
find: /media/cdrom: No medium found
find: /media/floppy: No medium found
```

This happens to be a common error; it's simply telling you that there was nothing found within those mounted drives.

Other errors you may encounter can range from problems accessing directories that you do not have permission to search, to completely obscure things that only senior Unix administrators may see. Always ask your system administrator for help if needed.

Learn How to Break In   Be careful when searching; you don't want to query the entire file system for something too generic, because you could be waiting a long time for those results to print on your screen. If you are stuck, you can try to break the sequence with a keystroke such as **[Ctrl+C]**. If this does not help, see your system administrator.

Finding a File by Its Date

In some cases, you may not be able to recall what a file is named or what its extension is, but you may know what day you created it. Creation date is another searchable criterion that you can select. To search, you will need to adapt a "how many days ago" mentality because Unix will search for files that have been made since the time that you specify. Let's look at an example:

1. Determine how many days ago your file was made.

2. Choose a starting directory for the search.

3. Use the find command with the -ctime option: find <starting directory> -ctime <how many days old> -print.

For example:

```
>find ~/ -ctime 5 -print
```

This command specifies that Unix should find a file in your home directory that is less than five days old and print it to the screen.

Now that you know how to find files using their creation date, let's learn how to find files by their size.

Finding a File by Its Size

In the previous examples, you used the find command to search for a file based on a specified location and to find a file based on its creation date. Both are good examples of searching for a good reason—you don't know where the file is! But why would you search for a file by its size? It may be easy to remember a name or when you worked on a file, but its size?

Believe it or not, there will be many times when you need to search a system for a file by its size. One great example is if you are a web designer and have large graphics files on your Unix system. Here, it's a great bet that these files will be larger than your word processor documents or spreadsheets.

To search by size, use the following steps:

1. Select a target file size, and `find` will locate all files of the selected size and larger.

2. Choose a starting directory.

3. Start the `find` program using the `-size` option: `find <starting directory> -size <k> -print`.

For example:

```
>find ~/ -size 1024k -print
/home/rob/updates/testgraphic.jpg
```

The `find` command you see here has located a graphics file that is larger than 1,024k.

 What Else Can You Find?   The `find` command is powerful. As you can see, using the `find` command with the `-name`, `-ctime`, and `-size` options can be helpful, but believe it or not, there is more.

Remember, with Unix, the power is at the command line. Use the man pages (as discussed in Lesson 2, "Getting Help") to learn other helpful options.

Finding Data with Other Unix Commands

In the previous section of this lesson we learned about the `find` command. When used, it can be powerful. Other commands you can use are `whereis` and `which`, and these commands may bring you results as well.

The `whereis` Command

The `whereis` command can be used to run a quick search on a specific number of directories for whatever you specify. For example, if you wanted to run a search on a file named "test", then you would get all instances of "test" that came up within that preset number of directories, such as paths to source code, binaries, and man pages. The whereis command performs a quick search for the file you specify.

```
>whereis test
test: /usr/bin/test /usr/share/man/man1/test.1.gz
/usr/share/man/man1p/test.1p.gz
```

Although this may not be exactly what you are looking for, this command can be useful.

The which Command

Another useful command is the which command. The which command can help you find files that are specified in your PATH environment variable. This was covered earlier in the book and will also be covered in Lesson 16, "Modifying Your Environment." This means that unless your data is specified in a location (such as a directory) within that PATH statement, you will not find it with use of the which command.

The which command is not useful in this scenario, but that does not mean that it can't be helpful. You may need to edit a file that you absolutely know is in your PATH statement and use this command to recall it quickly.

The grep Command

One of the most commonly used (and known) Unix commands is grep. Learning how to use grep will help you find files that contain a word or pattern. When the grep command is used properly, it can help you search through a file for something specific. For example, what if you wanted to search a file for a unique term?

When we talked about finding data on your Unix system, we narrowed the search down to different variables, such as the size of the file or the creation date. You can also narrow the search with grep.

You will soon learn that grep is one of the most powerful built-in programs in Unix. The program grep is also subdivided into more commands: grep, egrep, and fgrep. These three commands differ in what *regular expressions* they can handle. A regular expression is a pattern that can match various text strings. Regular expressions define a pattern of text that can be used to search files when a specific word or phrase to be searched for might not be known. To use grep,

1. Choose the word or phrase you want to find.

2. Find the filename you want to search.

3. Type **grep <pattern to find> <file or files to search>** at the shell prompt.

For example:

```
>grep "test" *.html
index.html:you passed the test
```

In this example, we see a quick grep of the word *test* in any file that resembles an HTML-based file. The grep command is a tool that will become even more valuable when you learn more about regular expressions.

Using the KDE Find Feature

If you are using the graphical user interface (GUI), then you will likely be using KDE. If so, then you can quickly search for files in KDE as well.

By going to the main menu and selecting Find Files, you will open a dialog box.

Once you see the dialog box, it should be self-explanatory. Instead of adding the commands you need (like find, whereis, and which), the Find Files dialog box will ask you what you are looking for (and where) and search that exact location for what you want.

This dialog box contains the same features of the command-line versions of find and grep. KDE has provided a GUI for these functions that make them easier to use. Again, you may prefer to use the shell prompt. The shell prompt helps you learn all the intricacies of the command, and the more commands you know, then the more scripting you will be able to handle when we get to Lesson 14, "Shell Scripting Fundamentals."

Now that you know and understand all the different utilities you can use, we will search for files on your Unix system with KDE. To search in the KDE, do the following:

1. Consider what file(s) you want to search for, and then click the **K** toolbar icon to bring up the main KDE menu.

2. Choose **Find Files**.

3. From the tabs you see, select what search criteria you want from three options: Name and Location, Date Modified, and Advanced. Consider using wildcards (*.rpm, for example) if you are unsure what to search for.

4. Click the small magnifying glass in the **Find Files** toolbar to locate the matching files.

To search for files, you can specify what file you want and then run your search. You can change where you are searching as well as what criteria you are searching for. Using the shell prompt commands or the KDE GUI, you can search using the following criteria: date, size, location, and name.

Now you should see the file you want. You can select the file and work with it, or you can just close the search. Either way, this concludes our discussion of how to find files within your Unix system.

Searching the Network With Unix, you may be connected to a network (which means you may have access to other systems), or you may just be using the local system where you have your files stored. If that's the case, then you can use every tool/command mentioned here and not worry about searching beyond the walls of your own hard disk or any other storage device directory connected to your Unix system. If you are connected to a network, be aware that when you search, it may take time because your search may be expanded past the local system. If you are unsure of whether the data you need is on your local system, ask your Unix administrator for help.

As we move into the next lesson, please remember what you have learned so far. Lessons build upon each other, so if you have any questions, you should review your work before moving forward. Unix mastery comes from doing things repetitively. Repetition builds memory, and before you know it, you will be rattling off Unix commands and amazing everyone with your shell-scripting skills. In the next lesson, we will cover how to perform basic file maintenance functions such as creating and deleting files and directories.

Summary

In this lesson we covered the fundamentals of finding files and directories within your Unix system as well as the different commands you can use. You also learned how to search the contents of a file itself with the grep command. In addition, you were introduced to finding files in the KDE GUI. Spend some time mastering the find and grep commands, and you will see that they are useful when you want to find data on your Unix system. We have skimmed only the surface of what grep can do once mastered. Visit the man page for grep and take a look at its power. Get comfortable using the man command; it can help you as well! Now that you can see that Unix provides a set of powerful utilities to help you find what you are looking for, you shouldn't feel like you are completely lost anymore, nor should your data.

- **find**—The find command can search the entire Unix file system or the area under any directory for a particular file based on a variety of criteria. You have seen how to use it to find files based on name, creation date, and size.

- **whereis**—If you're looking for a program file, its source, or its man pages, the whereis command might work for you. Searching a preset list of common file locations, whereis quickly returns paths to anything it finds.

- **which**—The which function is dependent on your PATH environment variable. It searches the paths that you have specified for a particular filename.

- **grep** (**grep/egrep/fgrep**)—The grep command set is an extremely powerful method of searching the actual content of files for a particular word or pattern. The power of the grep command when coupled with regular expressions (see Lesson 13, "Regular Expressions") is incredible.

- **Find Utility**—KDE provides an easy-to-use interface that encompasses many of the features of find and grep.

LESSON 6
Working with the Shell

In this lesson, you will expand on the last lesson and learn how to create and delete data from your Unix system.

In the last lesson we ended by talking about finding files within KDE. In this lesson, we focus primarily on the shell prompt and discuss how to manage data (files and directories) using the power of the Unix command line. We will also cover how to make directories and remove them.

Why would you want to do this? Well, there are many reasons. If you work with a very large amount of data, just having it organized in directories with names that correspond to your work or organization can save you a lot of time when trying to find data. As well, you may want to create a directory to put data in to send to someone so that it is organized. You may also need to delete a directory once it has been emptied, to save space, and again, to stay organized.

Deleting Needed Data Is Not Good There are a couple of things you should consider before using any of these commands in this lesson. Unix takes what you say very literally, so if you enter a command, be very careful. There are a couple of things you should consider before using any of these commands in this lesson.

You should not be tampering with production data at work if you are just practicing. You may want to ask for permission to work on your Unix system if you are afraid you may make a mistake and lose important data. If you are at home, the sky is the limit if you set up your system as a test system.

File management at the shell prompt is not difficult. In this next part of the lesson, we will cover the fundamentals of working with files and folders within Unix at the command line.

Working with Files at the Unix Shell Prompt

When working with Unix, you will most likely find it easiest to work with tools at the shell prompt. Using commands such as touch and rm is very helpful, and these commands perform different niche-based functions in much the same way as the whereis command covered in the last lesson. In Unix, there are multiple ways to create a file and edit it.

The command line is your primary interface to the Unix file system as well as your primary tool for creating, deleting, and rearranging your files. In this part of the lesson, we will learn how to manipulate data within the Unix system with the touch command as well as with commands used to help you remove newly created data on your Unix system.

The touch Command

Creating a new empty file in Unix is easy when you use the touch command. The touch command is used to update the last modified time of a file, setting it to the current time. This is usually not commonly used, but knowing about it can serve you well. The touch command is normally used with one particular area: backup and disaster recovery. As a Unix system administrator, you may be asked to do backup and restore jobs. There are a few different types (and methods) of backup and restore you can choose from, one of which is called an "incremental backup. Although this may not be something you work with in Unix, it is something you are most likely affected by. Most systems are backed up and protected by companies that need to save and keep their valuable data.

The touch command can be used with the incremental backup by helping to verify that a backup was in fact completed. Even if you never altered the data or modified it for any reason, you can still use the touch command to change the modification date and make it appear as if it had been modified, thus making it appear to have been modified at the time you touched it. This can be useful when you work with backups in particular, and you may also find other uses for it in your work with Unix.

 Where Did That New File Come From? When you "touch" a file by accident, you may wind up with a new file you may not have wanted. If you use the touch command and do not specify the actual filename (a file that really exists on your system), Unix will create a new file for you. For example, if you said you wanted to touch a file on your system named unixmaster, and it was really called unixmasters, then a unixmaster file will be created by Unix within the current directory you are working (or saving). You can do this by typing **pwd.**

Now that you understand the touch command, let's take a look at how you can use it. In this example we will look at both how to change the modification date of a file and how to make a new file altogether.

1. Determine the filename of the file or files you want to update or create.

2. Issue the touch command as touch *<filename>*.

For example, type

> **touch backupfile**

If the backup file previously existed, its last-modified date would now be set to the current time. If the backup file did not previously exist, it would now exist as an empty file with a last-modification date of the current time. It's that easy.

There are additional uses for the touch command. When you become comfortable enough with Unix to start automating your work using shell scripting (discussed in Lesson 14, "Shell Scripting Fundamentals"), you will find the touch command useful for creating "flag files" that allow your scripts to talk to each other. Keep the touch command in mind during Lesson 14.

Use Your Time Correctly   When working with Unix, (or any other operating system), you should have the correct time set on your system. This is usually done by a system administrator, as it's normally not done locally on the system. Instead, a time master is usually found somewhere on the network, from which your Unix system may pull the time. Of course, if your Unix system is not networked, then you will most likely be getting your correct time from the local system. Be aware of what time your Unix system says and where you are getting your time from.

Having your Unix system set with the proper time will help not only with file management, but also with logging and security.

Removing Files with the rm Command

If you used the touch command and now have a file that you do not want on your Unix system, you may want to get rid of it. In this next section, we will learn how to remove files from your Unix system.

The rm command is used to delete unwanted files on your Unix system. Remember that using this command can get you into some trouble if you don't use it properly—you could remove data from your system that you do not want to remove. Unix takes what you say very literally, so be careful—you are not in a Microsoft Windows environment that checks you every step of the way when you delete a file. If you want to remove a file from your Unix system, follow these steps to use the rm command:

1. Determine which file, or files, you want to delete.

2. Issue the rm command as rm *<filename>*.

As with using `touch`, `rm` is easy: As long as you can find and specify the filename, you can remove it.

 What If I Have Multiple Files? You can delete multiple files by leaving a space after each filename and then specifying the next. You can add or remove multiple files by specifying what files you want to add or remove, one after the other in tandem.

An example for using the following `rm` command:

```
rm newfile2
```

After issuing the `rm` command for the files you want to delete, you might be presented with a response such as

```
remove newfile (y/n)?
```

You can also use options with the `rm` command. Just like you used find with the `-print` option, you can use the `rm` command with its own set of options. Of course, you can use the man pages to learn more.

The `rm` command supports several useful options such as `-i`, `-f`, and `-r`. Each option will perform a different function when specified.

The "i" stands for interactive mode. The `-i` option makes `rm` ask you to confirm the deletion of each file before it is actually deleted.

Most Microsoft Windows users are familiar with this "safety checking" when you want to delete something. This `-i` option is how you can be absolutely sure you want to remove what you specified with the `rm` command in Unix.

Thus, the `rm` interactive mode is nothing more than a way for Unix to check with you to ensure that you really want to delete the data you specified. If you really want to remove the data, press **y**. This will take you back to the shell prompt, and your data will have been removed from the system.

The interactive mode will be configured by your Unix system administrator usually unless you are on a highly customized system.

The next option is rm using the -f option. The -f requests rm when you need to delete files that may have file permissions set on them. This option will allow you to remove the files without worrying about file permissions stopping the deletion process. Remember, you can create files and set the permissions on them so that even you can't read them. There will be times when using Unix where you may need to delete a file or files without having permission to read or write to them.

 Recursive Is Not a Curse Word in Unix   In this lesson we will discuss commands that, when used with a particular option, can perform recursive actions. What is that?

When relating to file management in Unix and the directory structure where Unix maintains its files and data, "recursive" means that when used, it will go through the directory from the starting point, down through all subdirectories, until it cannot search anymore.

The recursive actions are also repetitive; it will continue to search through each and every directory until the operation has been completed—it's an exhaustive command.

The last option we will discuss is the -r option, which stands for recursive. The -r option is a powerful option when using rm; the recursive mode can cause panic if you didn't intend to use it—so be careful. This command will remove the directory you specify, as well as anything that is contained within it, including other directories.

New Unix Mantra: Take a Quick Peek Before You Delete! The recursive option of the rm command is able to remove large amounts of data very quickly, so unless you have a backup handy, you may want to enter the directory you want to delete and use the ls command to see what is in the directory.

So now that we know how to create and delete files, let's look at another large aspect of file management within Unix: creating directories.

The mkdir Command

As mentioned earlier, directories are basically used to organize data. You may have experienced instances where you have one directory with hundreds of files. It would not be easy to find anything quickly unless you memorize every filename on your system.

Think of a phone book or telephone directory: The Unix directory is much the same. What if all businesses in your area were only listed in alphabetical order? How does that help you? How could you call an electrician, plumber, or anyone else unless you had groups of similar categories organized for quick retrieval? This is exactly why you need directories—for the simple organization of data on your Unix system. In this part of the lesson, we will learn to make directories.

To make a directory, you can do the following:

1. Choose an organizational structure, and name your new directory.

2. Issue the mkdir command as mkdir *<directoryname>*.

For example:

```
> mkdir test
```

This creates a new directory named test, which will be located in the current directory. To find the current directory you are in, you can issue the pwd command, and then the mkdir command. Doing an ls will show you the contents. So, now that you know how to make a directory, you will need to know how to delete it from your Unix system as well.

The rmdir Command

The rmdir command will delete an empty directory. What this means is that the directory you want to remove cannot contain any data within it.

To remove a directory, do the following:

1. Decide which directory, or directories, you want out of your way.

2. Issue the rmdir command as rmdir <directory>.

 Don't Forget! You Can Do Many At Once! Don't forget that you can remove multiple directories at one time. As with most file management commands, specify the directories in sequence and they will be removed. For example, if you wanted to remove "test" and "test1," the two directories could be removed with one issuance of the rmdir command. You could rmdir "test" and "test1" by typing **rmdir test test1**.

When you issue the rmdir command, you will remove the test directory you created before:

```
> rmdir test
```

That's it! That was pretty easy to do. You should now be able to list the contents in your current directory and not see the test directory anywhere. It has been removed. If you had any problems, you may need to make the directory you want to remove from the Unix system "empty." In some cases, you must use rm * first to make the directory empty, and then you can delete it. As this is advanced syntax better covered in Lesson 13,

"Regular Expressions," when we cover regular expressions, you should put this * symbol (known as the asterisk, or wildcard) to memory, as you will most likely often use this command when working with Unix.

Now that we have mastered file creation and deletion, as well as directory creation and deletion, you should learn what combinations are most commonly used and helpful, as well as know the answers to the most commonly asked questions: Why would I make a directory empty before deleting it? Couldn't I delete the directory with the files in it? Yes, you may do so with the rm -r (recursive) command.

What Is This? The Same Command?   Just like the remove files command, the recursive command is pretty much the same command—it just does something different when used in a different context (as in the context of directories), not files. When used this way, you can recursively remove all of the contents within that directory you specify.

The rm -r Command

Removing files and directories at the same time can be done when using the rm -r command specifying a directory instead of a file. The rmdir command will only work on empty directories, so you will need a way to remove the directory and any contents that may be within it. When you need this functionality, the rm command in recursive mode can be used.

To delete a directory and all its contents, do the following:

1. Find the directory you want deleted.

2. Issue the rm command as rm -r <directoryname>.

When you issue this command, you will be able to specify the directory you want to delete, including anything that may be in it:

```
> rm -r /priv/home/rob/test2
```

If you delete a directory you are currently in, you may get error messages. These may be fixed easily by moving to a known good directory, such as your home directory, symbolized by the tilde. The command you can enter to get back to home is **cd** *~/*.

Wow, think about how far you have come! Not only are we navigating the Unix shell prompt, we are actually making and removing data from the Unix system, as well as becoming more familiar with how other commands tie in to the process. Now we will learn how to copy files from one location to another.

The cp Command

When you want to make a copy of a file, you can use the cp command. The cp command will allow you to copy a single file to a new destination file, or copy one or more files to a single destination directory. This file operation will come up many times in your workings with Unix. It's not uncommon to want to make copies of files you are working on. If you wanted to make a quick backup copy of a file, this command could help you do that.

To use the cp command to make a copy of a single file, follow these steps:

1. Determine the source filename, and the destination filename to which you'd like to copy the file.

2. Issue the cp command as cp *<sourcefile>* *<destinationfile>*.

There will be times where you may not have just one file, but perhaps a dozen files that you want to send to a particular directory. To do this, you would issue the cp command with the multiple source files listed to one directory.

To use the cp command to copy multiple files to a destination directory, you would change the command as follows:

1. Issue the cp command as cp <sourcefile1> <sourcefile2> [...] <destinationdirectory>.

To see an example of this in action, type the command

```
> cp testfile /priv/home/rob/storage
```

The example shown here copies the file testfile from the current directory and places the copy in /priv/home/rob/storage. This would be commonly done if you were working in an environment in which you would work on a file and then send it to a local storage point on your Unix system, maybe in your home directory, for organizational purposes. You may have in your storage folder three other subfolders such as spreadsheet, document, and HTML. This is commonly practiced, and you may want to adopt this technique into your own work environment for your organizational needs.

Back to our example for copying files, if you wanted to send multiple files to your HTML folder, you may do something like this:

```
> cp /priv/home/rob/index.htm /priv/home/rob/test/banner.htm
links.htm /priv/home/rob/storage/HTML
```

When using the cp command in this fashion, you are telling Unix to copy index.htm from the /priv/home/rob directory, which is where it was saved last, as well as both banner.htm and links.htm from the /priv/home/rob/test directory, and place them all in the /priv/home/rob/storage/HTML directory.

Now that you have learned the copy command, truly master it by reading the man page and making sure you know all the other things you can do with it. Next, we will learn how to copy directories.

The cp -r Command

Now that you have learned the fundamentals of copying files, what about directories? As we have learned with other commands in this lesson, the recursive option is very powerful, so when it is used in this application, it will allow you to copy multiple directories, subdirectories, and files to a destination directory of your choice.

The cp command has a recursive mode for copying directories. When it is used with the following syntax, the cp command with the -r option, you will be able to copy each source directory (as well as files) into whatever destination directory you specify. An example of this would be as follows:

1. The data to be copied to the destination directory must be specified.

2. Issue the cp command as cp -r <sourcedirectory1> <sourcedirectory2> [...] <destinationdirectory>.

Performing this action will take whatever you specify as the source and copy it recursively to the destination directory, as seen in the following example:

```
> cp -r /priv/home/rob/storage/HTML /etc/HTMLLAB
```

This command will copy the /priv/home/rob/storage/HTML directory and its contents into the /etc/HTMLLAB directory. This copied HTML and a subdirectory named IMAGES into the /etc/HTMLLAB directory, thanks to the recursive option.

In this part of the lesson, we covered using the recursive option with the cp command. You can now copy directories as well. Let's take a look at moving files and directories.

The mv Command

Moving files is not like copying them. Copying them leaves the source of the data in the original location in addition to creating a duplicate copy in another location, or in the same location with a different name. To move a file or directory, you need to use the mv command. The mv command will move or rename a file based on the destination. Depending on what you specify as the destination, the filename is going to specify how you used the command.

In other words, look at the following two examples of the mv command:

1. Locate a file you want to move by its filename. This is the source file you want to move.

2. Issue the mv command as mv <sourcefile> <directory>.

When used in this fashion, the command will move the selected file to the directory you want it to be in. You can also issue the same command to rename a file. It will also leave the source alone; however, when it copies the file (you can even do this to the same source directory), it is new and the contents are identical. To Unix, there are two completely different files located in the same directory.

To rename a file is not land keep it in the same source directory, issue the mv command as mv *<currentname>* *<newname>*.

Why could it not be in the same source directory unless you renamed it? Well, then it would be two instances of the same thing in one directory, and Unix will not allow for that—nor any other operating system. For the file system to be able to manage itself, having duplicate entries in the same source without a way to distinguish the two is not only impossible, but useless—if you edit one, then when you save it (besides for some file size changes), how would you know which is which?

You can do the same exercise with directories as well—just specify directories instead of filenames.

 Where Did I Put That Thing?   If you move something, you could lose it. So you must be careful and think through your actions. You could inadvertently move data that could ruin a website, or disable a service or application.

Copy is always your best choice, but then you pile up data on your hard disk. If you are not thinking about your actions, you could add storage stresses with unnecessary copying or disable your system by moving something you should have copied. Pay attention and if you make a mistake, contact your Unix system administrator for help, or revert to some of the older commands you learned to help you find what you need.

Let's take a quick look at the mv command in action:

```
> mv /priv/home/rob/storage/HTML/index.htm /etc/HTMLAB
```

Remember, this will move the source you specify (index.htm) to the HTMLAB directory located in the /etc directory. It's that simple. What if you wanted to move more than one source to a destination? That would be common, much like using the cp command; in that case, you would specify more source files to move.

To move multiple files to a directory, do the following:

```
> mv /priv/home/rob/storage/HTML/index.htm
/priv/home/rob/storage/HTML/GRAPHICS/b1.jpg b2.jpg /etc/HTMLLAB
```

This moves the index.htm from the /HTML directory as well as a couple of JPEGs (image files) to the /HTMLLAB directory within the /etc directory.

Before we end this part and move on, there is one limitation to the mv command that you need to know about. In a previous lesson, we discussed the fact that you may have data stored locally on your system, and you may have a network connection to other Unix systems that you may access for data. You accessing their local data would mean that you are accessing that data remotely. If you access data remotely, you may have issues with the mv command. Because the mv command cannot move directories between physical devices, you may need to copy the file from one location to another, and then delete the original. Up to now, we have learned all the commands needed to complete such an operation, shown here in this example of transferring data over a network.

Now that we have learned how to copy and move directories, we will do our last exercise of this lesson: learn how to create links. Remember, we discussed links in Lesson 5, "File System Navigation Techniques," when we saw files "linked" to others.

The ln Command

As discussed previously in this book, when you learn the ls command, you should be aware of "links" to other files when you list out the contents of a directory. Those links can be made with the ln command.

The ln command is used to build links or aliases to other files on your Unix system. You can create manageable links to other files so that they can appear in the ls command output when you want the source file to appear to be in different locations, as well as have different names.

Practical application of this command would allow a source file that constantly changed names to be linked to a name that everyone could remember. For instance, a file named sales_report that all marketing managers could access may be kept up to date by a secretary who links a series of dated files to sales_report. The managers only need to remember one name, instead of having to remember multiple names, or having to constantly find or request what that name would be. It's a way to make things easier for you while working with Unix.

To create a link, do the following:

1. Specify the particular file you want to link to another file. The ln command will create a link from the source file to an alternative name for that file to be accessed. You need to know the original name and then the name you want it to be referenced by.

2. Issue the ln command as ln -s <realfilename> <alternatename>.

3. Issue the ls -l command to view the long listing and the link you created.

When using the ln command, you need to be very specific about creating a link. Take care not to make the mistake of specifying a filename that doesn't exist and then creating a link to it—it will be useless and not link to anything. You should view the original source filename and make sure that when you build a link that you specify the exact filename to avoid this error.

Another issue you may face involves forgetting to use the -s option. The -s option is nothing more than specifying that you want to create a soft link instead of a hard link. Since hard links are not really used by Unix end users, we will not dig too deeply into the meanings here, as it's a bit beyond the scope of this book and not likely to be anything you will see or use as a novice user of Unix. As I mentioned earlier in this book, it's imperative that you take the initiative to dig into these topics deeper on your own if you are interested in all that you can do with Unix—keep learning and practicing as much as you possibly can.

An example of the `ln` command to create a link can be seen here:

```
> ln -s /priv/home/rob/storage/HTML/123456789ABC.htm /etc/
HTMLLAB/easy
```

If you were to do this, you would create a link named "easy" in the HTMLLAB directory that would be linked to the very long and not easy to remember HTML file located in your stored HTML directory.

That's it! That's creating a link, and now you not only know how to do it, but a practical reason why you should. Our last discussion in this lesson focuses on the proper way of using relative or absolute paths.

Knowing the Right Path

We discussed the difference between relative and absolute paths in Lesson 5. By managing data using commands such as `cp` and `mv`, you can also specify different paths when issuing the command. There are shortcuts and other tips (that could fill 50 of these books) that can help you be more productive.

It is very important to remember that when you give a filename as an argument to a Unix command, the filename can be either a relative or absolute path to the file. Consider this when you type out your command. Sometimes you may not be specifying the command properly and that is why it's failing; for example, if relative and absolute paths either use / or not, this may cause you to issue the command incorrectly and possibly give you an error message. If this happens, review the previous lesson on paths and apply that knowledge to your commands as you continue to learn and use them.

Summary

In this lesson you learned more file management skills, which will serve as building blocks for the next few chapters in which you will learn to read and edit files.

At this point, you should be able to log into your Unix system and manage the locally stored data on it, and to move, copy, and delete data files.

In the next lesson we will learn how to read files and continue to build our Unix file management and navigational skills so that you can work with Unix more productively.

In this lesson you learned a set of flexible set of Unix commands that will allow you to manage the data stored on your system.

The following is a quick review of this lesson:

- **touch**—The touch command sets the modification date of the file to the current time. This has the effect of creating new empty files if you need them.

- **rm**—The rm command removes files. Use the rm -i option until you are quite certain that you know what you are doing, and then keep using it for a while longer. Recursive rm running in non-interactive mode can wipe out your entire disk.

- **cp**—The cp command copies one or more files. Although a slight oversimplification, it's easiest to remember that if you start with a single file, your destination needs to be a single file; if you start with multiple files, your destination must be something that can hold multiple files (such as a directory). You can also copy a single file to a directory if you want to.

- **mv**—The mv command works a lot like cp, only it renames or moves files. The mv command cannot move directories across physical hardware boundaries, so every now and then Unix's hardware abstraction fails with this command. If this happens, look to the cp command for help.

- **ln**—The ln command creates alternative names by which a file or directory can be accessed. It's convenient for times when you need one file to appear to be in several different places, or when you need to make information that comes from different files at different times all appear under the same filename.

LESSON 7
Reading Files

In this lesson we discuss how to read files located on your Unix system.

We will continue to learn about file management and continue to build upon the concepts learned in earlier lessons. In this lesson we will look at a few handy commands that will help you to read data within a file. That doesn't sound too exciting, now does it? Well, actually it is exciting, because if you haven't used Unix for file management before (or in a limited manner), you may not want to go back to anything else! In Unix, you have the power to look at large files in sections. For example, if you have a security log on your Unix system that must be read every morning, you can use a particular command to just look at the last entries in the log.

You know how to manage files—that was the hard part to learn; now we just need to know how to read the data you have stored on your Unix system without a GUI-based text editing tool or a word processor. In this chapter we look at some helpful tools that take only a second to use and increase your productivity. You will be spending less time working within a cumbersome GUI, because you can just type a quick command like cat and have the information you need in seconds.

The cat Command

When learning Unix, it's common to first learn the cat command. An easy abbreviation to remember if you are pet friendly, this command will concatenate the elements you specify into one package. The easiest way to look at files is to use cat, the *concatenate* command.

Concatenated, What's That? Most words in the computer industry can be overwhelming to learn because most of what you hear is acronym based, defined in a complicated way, and so on. In this case, the word concatenate is nothing more than the theory of combining elements for efficiency sake.

In Unix, we use concatenates because Unix has the capability to string or place together two or more files to create a single file. Data elements (strings) and contents (files) can be combined together into a new element or file. Think of concatenation as the ability to combine things together for ease of use.

The cat command is a byproduct of this definition. The cat command will allow you to concatenate all data specified together into one package.

Now that you are comfortable with the definition and what cat does, let's look at the operation of the cat command. Now, there are a couple of ways to use the cat command. We will look at it in the light of reading files and will touch on it in Lesson 12, "Input and Output," later in the book. Until then, let's just focus on using cat to read files on your system.

To display a file, just supply cat with the file(s) you want to see. If you want to see how powerful Unix is, cat a file like the b1.jpg (JPEG image file). Unix will look inside it and report back to you. Unix will report in a language you can't read or understand, but this shows you that Unix is literal in everything you ask it to do. Unix will do it or crash and die trying!

One example that I am sure you will be able to find on your system is your hosts file located in your /etc directory. I have left out most of the output as the hosts file can be quite large, but this is exactly one of the main benefits of the cat command. I didn't need to do anything but specify the cat command and either the directory (if I am not in it) and the file.

```
>cat hosts
#
# hosts      This file describes a number of hostname-to-
address_____
#           mappings for the TCP/IP subsystem. It is
_____
#           mostly used at boot time, when no name servers are
running._____
#           On small systems, this file can be used instead of a
Named name server.
# Syntax:
# IP-Address Full-Qualified-Hostname Short-Hostname
#

127.0.0.1  localhost

(Output removed)
```

In this example, while in our /etc directory, we used the cat command to view the hosts file for its current entries. We had only one entry because I removed the long stream of output. This can be seen with other commands that we will learn about shortly in this lesson. With cat, you can easily and quickly see the contents of a file.

Another item of importance is that you must know what you can and can't use cat with. The cat command will return an error message to you if you try to cat a directory. The error message will tell you that you are trying to cat a directory and that this is not allowed. Be aware that cat is for files, not for directories. You can also specify multiple filenames. However, when you receive the results back from your query, you will be given a longer list of the combined concatenates. Do not specify any directories when specifying multiple filenames with the cat command or your query may fail. Also make sure that you test out your wildcards and attempt to build them into your cat command queries. For instance, if you want to search for all the files in your /etc directory that may be hosts files, run a query on it, narrow down your search criteria, and cat the file you want to see. You can also cat multiple files.

You can cat all the files simultaneously, but the query results would be so large that your results would scroll off the screen too quickly for you to

even digest the first sentence shown. Having said that, let's still look at a
way to view the entire result so you don't miss anything. First find what
you want to look at:

```
>find host*
hosts
hosts.conf
hosts.allow
hosts.deny
```

Since my query specified looking for host*, everything that starts with
the word host will be shown with whatever comes after it because of the
use of the wildcard. You can then cat your files to see which one is
relevant for use.

```
>cat host*
```

This will show you more output than you can possibly even read. We will
now move on to managing what you view in a better way, so you can
actually read the data! You can use pagers to slow down the output to
make it readable.

Making Output Readable with Pagers

The cat command is fine when you just want to quickly show some information, but what about large files that scroll past a bit too quickly to read
and you now can't read them? There is a way to slow down the output of
a command like cat, so you can read the data at your speed. Viewing
pages one at a time is done with the concept of pagers. Files that scroll off
the screen will be useless if you need to read the beginning of the file. If
the file's size is larger than what can fit on the terminal screen or in your
history buffer, you are out of luck. Files are often large enough to do this,
and you will still want to read those files. You can use new Unix commands. You can use more and less. People often refer to more and less
by their generic term: pagers. Let's take a quick look at how to use these
command-line tools.

The more Command

All you need to do to use more is to type the command followed by the
file or files you want to display. This command is similar to cat. The
tricky part is memorizing when to use which and having that knowledge
at your fingertips when you need it most. Let's take a look at the more
command in action:

```
>more hosts.allow
(Output removed)
```

For this command you will need to have a file that is long enough to
scroll off your screen and warrants the use of the command. If you type in
the wrong command, or you specify a file that is not long enough to scroll
off the screen, more will more or less do nothing for you. (Pun intended.)

When you use the more command with a long file, you immediately see
something new on your terminal screen. On the bottom left of the screen,
you will see the more command in action:

```
--More--(53%)
```

Fifty-three percent is what you have seen and the rest is what still needs
to be seen. You know from the percentage how many pages you are dealing with. If you had 25%, then it's three or four pages of output to view.

Pressing the **Spacebar** will bring you to the next page. You can use the **q**
on the keyboard to quit the program, or **Ctrl+z** will also stop the more
command if you want to break the sequence of using it. Using **s** on the
keyboard will skip one line at a time and is helpful to use if you want to
scroll through your output line by line, instead of page by page.

In this section we looked at how to use more to page through your output.
Using cat showed you contents of a file, but you had little control over
being able to view large files and this is where the more command is
useful. Now, let's take a look at the less command, which is a new
version of the more command. So you can do more with less!

Less Is More, Literally   The meanings can actually be reversed for some computer terms, as in the case of using the commands `less` and `more`.

Using `less` is a newer binary that can really help you page through output better, and it is frequently used by Unix systems administrators. Therefore, it is highly probable that you already have this installed on your machine.

The `less` Command

Using the `less` command is similar to using the `cat` and `more` commands. As a matter of fact, the syntax is nearly identical. It's really what the tool does that makes it different. When using the `less` command, you have more control over the pager than ever before.

Here is a good example of the differences between `more` and `less`:

```
>more hosts.allow
```

If you try to use the arrow keys for navigation while using the `more` command, you will find that you can only move forward through the file with the **Spacebar**. There is not a back and forth as there is with the `less` command. Now try the same things using the `less` command.

```
>less hosts.allow
```

You can move up and down through the file using your arrow keys. You can even move to the right buffer if you are working on a terminal emulation program like telnet or secure shell. Either way, if you are connected to a Unix system and can use `more` or `less`, check them out and see what they can do for you. Other options that come with `less` are similar to those that come with `cat` and `more`. The **Spacebar** always moves you through the file via the page, and **q** will give you the ability to quit out of the program.

Ask for It   If you are not using the less command at work and think it may be more productive for you, request it.

Now that you are comfortable with the fundamentals on how to read a file with cat, more, and less, there may be times when you only need to look at a section of a file. You may have a need to look at the bottom of a log file, or at the top of an email message header to get the source and destination addressing out of it. If you do not need to look at a complete file and just need to look at a section of it, then you can use the head and tail commands.

The tail Command

The tail command is simple to remember. If you want to see the tail end of a file, use the tail command. If you want to see the top, use the head command. Now that you know the simplicity in remembering them, let's look at what each does starting with tail.

The tail command is powerful, quick, and simple to use. If you want to see the bottom 10 lines of a file, then you may want to just specify the tail command and the file you want to view the inside of.

```
>tail hosts.allow
```

Or

```
>tail -20 hosts.allow
```

The output of this command starts from the bottom up and displays (by default) 10 lines from the bottom up. If you specify the amount of lines you want to see, count the amount of lines from the bottom up and that is what you will view.

The inverse of this command is the head command. As mentioned earlier, the head is the top and you want to use the head command to show you the beginning of the file.

The head Command

In some instances you may need to see the top of a file just like you may
have needed to see the bottom of a file. To use the head command, do the
same as you would with the tail command.

>head hosts.allow

Or

>head -20 hosts.allow

The output of this command starts from the top down (not the bottom up)
and displays (by default) 10 lines from the top down instead of the
bottom up.

Heads or Tails? Let's Flip for It!   A good tip to
remember when using head and tail is that when you
are changing the default number of lines shown from
10, specify the amount of lines you do want to see.
This can be done with the -# option that we just
previously touched on.

Remember, you can always use the help command or
man pages to learn more about any command on
your Unix system. If you'd like to change the number
of lines that are displayed by default, you can override
it with the use of -#. In this command, # is the number
of lines you would like to view.

That wraps up our lesson on using the shell prompt to read files. There are
more commands and options you can use, but as with anything in Unix,
the amount you can do just keeps expanding as you open new doors. For a
book this size, we have to cap what is covered to some degree. Make sure
not to forget that Lesson 2, "Getting Help," shows you how to gather help.
Continue to build up your skill level and experience using Unix. For file
management, make sure you know how to read files using cat, more,
less, head, and tail.

Summary

Reading files in your Unix system can be done very easily. Working via the command prompt can be difficult but by now, that difficulty level should be diminishing and fading away as you learn more and more about Unix. In this lesson we learned how to work with Unix files and read them via many shell prompt tools. This lesson should have given you a clear picture of the many different ways you can display files, or portions of files.

Here's a review:

- **cat**—This concatenate command displays all the files you specify, one after the other. It does not pause at the end of pages.

- **more/less**—These are known as pagers. They page through their input files, one screen at a time. less offers the ability to scroll backwards through files unlike more. more provides forward-only viewing.

- **head**—Displays the first few lines of a file. This is useful when you're trying to look at header information in files such as email messages.

- **tail**—Views the end of a file. Used with the -f option, tail provides the useful capability of displaying a logfile as it is generated. Rather than each program needing its own monitoring utility, tail -f can be used instead.

- **Other file formats**—Although many Unix information files are text or HTML based, there are other formats that you might encounter. This lesson looked briefly at some of those formats, and the programs that you can use to work with them.

LESSON 8
Text Editing

In this lesson you will learn the basics of editing files at the shell prompt and in the GUI within the Unix environment.

Now that we have discussed the reading of files we need to know how to edit them as well. In this chapter we cover the basics of file editing in two environments: the shell prompt and using the GUI. Editing files is common in any environment. Whether you are an author who has to master text-editing tools or just a novice typing an email, knowing how to edit files is a very important skill to have.

In this chapter we will look at the two most commonly used file-editing programs today within a Unix environment: the vi editor and emacs. The vi editor is used at the shell prompt, and emacs is used within the GUI.

So, now that you know how to read files in many different ways, it's time to learn how to create and edit them using these tools.

Master Your Weapon! It would simply be impossible to cover the endless things that you can do with both programs; they truly are very dense and have a great many tools within them. If you are going to move on and try to master Unix, it may help you to master a text-editing tool because you will find yourself using them a lot in Unix.

In this lesson we will dig as deep as we can into both editors, yet we will still barely skim the surface. We will introduce you to the basics of how to edit files, create them, and save them. We will also cover basic navigation and a few other tips as well.

Text Editing with Unix

Text editing is a common thing to do in any environment. For instance, most websites and their associated web pages run on Unix or Linux web servers. This is a fact. That being said, think of what a website is comprised of. A website contains directories and files that create a website. This is what you would commonly access with a web browser. I am sure you already know this, but what you may not know is that those files saved in the HTML format are nothing more than files that you can edit. Once edited, those files will display whatever it is you desire to configure.

All of this can be done by default with any standard installation of Unix or Linux with either the vi editor or emacs. Create a document and save it with a .htm extension (for HTML or Hypertext Markup Language format) and you save it to a directory that you set up for the web as a website. It's that simple; you have just created your first web page.

Can you see the power of the text editor now? That's not all. You will be amazed at what these tools can do, and the sheer power they contain will keep you learning for what seems a lifetime.

There is some humor in learning about editing files within Unix as well. There is actually a rivalry between groups who think vi editor is better than emacs and vice versa. Regardless of which is better, one thing is for certain: Unix editors have immense power, so it's certain that no matter which one you happen to choose, you will be happy. Commonly, those used to shell prompts and older Unix users and administrators prefer the vi editor. Those who use GUI environments are more used to working with emacs.

In this lesson we cover both. My recommendation to you is that whichever one makes you happy, dig deeper into it beyond this pocket guide that covers only the fundamentals.

The vi Editor

The vi editor is by far one of the most used editors in the Unix community today. The vi editor has been around for a long time and continues to find new fans at an increasing rate. It's a streamlined, highly functional tool that does not require much memory. It can be said that the vi editor is Unix's most universal editor. Pronounced *vee-eye*, vi isn't a user-friendly editor. In fact, one of the hardest things to learn and master in Unix is file editing with the vi editor. The power of the vi editor comes from its low overhead and high functionality.

To use the vi editor, you only need to open it up using the vi command. To see the vi editor in action, do the following:

1. Select a file you want to edit with the vi editor.

2. Issue the vi command as vi *<filename>*.

 Create Files with Ease Using vi!   You can open the vi editor without specifying a file you want to edit. This will then create a new file for you that once saved, will show you that the vi editor is a good tool to use.

To see the vi editor in action editing a preexisting file, type the following command:

```
> vi /etc/HTMLLAB/index.htm
```

This will open up the vi editor and the file opened will be the website's home page, index.htm. You may not have this same file; if not, use the find command to locate a file you would like to edit or view with the vi editor and open it.

Now that you have a file opened, you can use a plethora of commands to edit the file. If you do have an HTML document open, you need to know how to edit HTML code to create changes on a website. If you have a file open, you may be able to read a help file for a specific application installed on your system. No matter what you choose, you will find the vi editor has a wide array of commands that can be used within it to work with the open files. One thing you have to consider is what mode the vi editor is working in. There are two modes that the vi editor operates in. The vi editor either uses command mode or insert mode.

- **Command mode**—You can control things such as cursor position, deleting characters, and saving files.

- **Insert mode**—You can insert characters.

Now that you know how vi operates, let's use it. To open a file is easy, but to actually edit it and then save it is a whole different set of tasks that we need to learn and master. You have to know how to edit files and that comes from mastering the vi editor's basic operation. Mastering the vi editor comes only from mastering the keyboard shortcuts used to operate the vi editor. Table 8.1 shows the most common manipulation keyboard shortcuts you will use.

TABLE 8.1   Common vi Keyboard Actions

Mode	Key(s)/Key Combination(s)	Action
Command	**l**	Move right
	h	Move left
	j	Move to the next line
	k	Move to the previous line
	Put cursor on the character to delete and then press the **x** key	Delete a character
	Press the **d** key twice	Delete an entire line (including to delete an empty line)
	Position cursor on the line to append and press **A**	Append the end of a line

continues

TABLE 8.1   Continued

Mode	Key(s)/Key Combination(s)	Action
	i (before the character under the cursor) or **a** (after the character under the cursor)	Changes to insert mode
	:w Return	Save the file
	:w<filename>	Save the file to a new name
	:q Return	To exit vi
	:q! Return	Quit without saving
Insert mode	**Esc** key	Changes to command
	Backspace and **Delete** keys	Backspaces or deletes, but only for data just inserted

This is not a complete list; we could probably fill this little pocket guide full of 10 minute lessons with what you can do with the vi editor from the keyboard. Perhaps it would be beneficial to visit your local library and take out a book on the vi editor to learn more ways to make it work for you, not against you.

Remember that this book can only cover so much so it is important that you be careful editing files and stepping beyond the basics in the current Unix environment you are in. Set up a test lab if possible and explore from there; you will find it easier to learn and work that way.

This is an example of how you can use the vi editor to edit a file named test. The two commands you need to perform this exercise are **Return**, which will move to a new line of text, and **Esc**, which is how you escape. Now, make a new file called test:

```
> vi test
This is a new file I created!
Check it out,
Isn't it snazzy?
I thought it was
```

By doing this, Unix will respond back to you with

```
"test" [New file] 4 lines, 61 characters
```

If you remember how to use the `cat` command, you can quickly view the contents of the new file you created call `test`.

```
> cat test
This is a new file I created!
Check it out,
Isn't it snazzy?
I thought it was
```

As you can see, the `vi` editor can be helpful to you for editing a plethora of different file types. Make sure you remember that learning the `vi` editor takes a lot of time and practice. I hope that you continue to use it; if not, then maybe you might like to try `emacs`.

The `emacs` Editor

Most `emacs` lovers hate `vi` and vice versa. Why such rivalry? Well, I hope that you have yet to be tainted by someone else's opinions. I hope that you can make a decision on your own from this Unix lesson alone. Take a look at both and form your own opinion on what can be most useful to you and learn how to use that tool as in-depth as you can. In this lesson, we will look at the `emacs` editor.

You will find that the biggest difference between the `emacs` editor and the `vi` editor is the actual footprint of the programs. Whereas the `vi` editor is a lightweight, highly functional tool, the `emacs` editor is a dense, unbelievably functional tool. Don't worry, both will serve just about any need you can dream of; most times the selection is preference. Very few get to levels where they know so much about both that they can rattle off verbatim all the differences and why you would want to use one over the other in specific circumstances. The easiest way to make a decision if you are completely new to Unix is to consider again that the vi editor is functional and very lightweight. The vi editor doesn't eat up a lot of your computer's hardware resources like memory and CPU cycles. The emacs editor, however, can be resource intensive and actually tax your system, making it perform slower if too many resources are used. This is because emacs contains a great many things such as an email client, a programming language, and many other features.

In a more technical light, emacs is by far more functional than vi, but again, it all depends on what you are looking for. For the price of functionally, you pay the cost of resource consumption. Life is a give and take, so is Unix running on your workstation's hardware. When we covered the vi editor, we covered its mode. When using emacs, you are always in insert mode. Control (**Ctrl** key) functions are handled by using **Ctrl** key sequences instead of a separate mode. We will cover these momentarily. Now that you understand the differences when using emacs and how it operates, let's take a look at how to use the editor:

1. Choose a file you would like to open and edit.

2. Issue the emacs command as emacs *<filename>*.

That's it; it's that easy to do. Once opened, the emacs editor is very similar to the vi editor in that you will manipulate the file's contents, save it, and so on.

Create Files with Ease Using emacs Too!　Just like the vi editor, you can open the emacs editor without specifying a file you want to edit; this will then create a new file for you.

Once emacs opens, you will see many ways to get help. Although you can explore on your own, it's suggested you know some basic navigation first; emacs is just as tricky as vi is to get around and takes a little practice first.

Know Your Syntax In the following list, whenever you see **Ctrl+** preceding a character, it means that you need to hold down the **Control (Ctrl)** key and type that character.

Learning and using the emacs editor can be difficult, but here are some tips to help you navigate it and learn it:

- As mentioned earlier, the emacs editor doesn't have a separate mode for entering commands. There is only one mode and you use the control keys to move to what would be considered another mode. You are always either typing a command or typing text—no switching modes between them like the vi editor. To type text, you just need to type it; if you need to enter a command, you can use the control key to do this, usually seen as **Ctrl+option**.

- You can position the cursor keys in emacs by using the arrow-key keypad in most every version of emacs and terminal combination. This is handy if you are new to learning how to get around emacs. The emacs editor is easy to use once you master the keyboard shortcuts, just like the vi editor. If the arrow keys don't work, you can also position the cursor by using **Ctrl+f** to move forward, **Ctrl+b** to move backwards, **Ctrl+p** to move to the previous line, and **Ctrl+n** to move to the next line.

- You can delete everything from the cursor to the end of the current line by pressing **Ctrl+k**.

- **Ctrl+g** is the emacs "quit what you're doing" command. If you've started typing a command and change your mind, then use **Ctrl+g**.

- If you use **Ctrl+k** to delete a line or lines, you can press **Ctrl+y** to yank them back again.

- To save the file you're currently editing, press **Ctrl+x Ctrl+s**.

- To save the file to a new filename, press **Ctrl+x Ctrl+w** <*filename*>**Return**.

- To exit emacs press **Ctrl+x Ctrl+c**. If emacs asks you about unsaved buffers or saving your work, you can select Yes to the "quit anyway?" question and to save your work.

Beyond the set of **Ctrl+** commands that you can use within the emacs editor, the **Escape** key can also add more functionality if needed. These commands are usually known as emacs *meta* commands for historical reasons.

Although they're too complicated and too specific to cover in this book, access to many of the interesting emacs meta commands is accomplished by pressing **Esc x**, and then typing a command of some sort, such as **info**. The editor will then give you a list of all commands with similar names for you to choose from. You can see that you will find what you need from the list for most situations.

> **Use the emacs Tutorial**   If someone offered you a free pot of gold, would you take it? Of course, but what about if they offered you free help on emacs? Yeah, I know, you would pass on it. What fun is there in that?
>
> Although not the most fun, you can take the emacs tutorial to help get a jump on learning it.
>
> To enter the emacs tutorial, all you need to do is start emacs, and press **Ctrl+hi** (hold the **Ctrl** key down, press **h**, release the **Ctrl** key, and press **i**). If you type a **?** after the **Ctrl+h** instead of the **i** you'll see that there's actually a whole world of alternatives to the **i**; these alternatives give you a large range of different types of helpful information.

Now that you have learned how to edit the files at the shell prompt, let's dive into the GUI and learn how to edit files in KDE.

Desktop Environment Tools: KDE's Built-in Editor

The graphical environment also provides a built-in editor that is very powerful. Many environments, such as KDE, will provide you with a mouse click environment to work in while working with your files. Just like if you were working with Apple Macintosh or Microsoft Windows, you can expect the Unix GUI to also provide the same functionality.

In this part of the lesson we will move away from the shell prompt for a moment and work within the GUI. To activate the KDE editor click on the **K** in the KDE toolbar. Now, choose **Applications** from the pop-up menu, and then **Editor** from its submenu. Depending on the distribution of Unix you are using, you may not have this exact layout, but you will most likely be familiar with basic navigation such as finding what would resemble the start menu within a Windows environment.

Once you open KDE's editor, you will see what is shown in Figure 8.1.

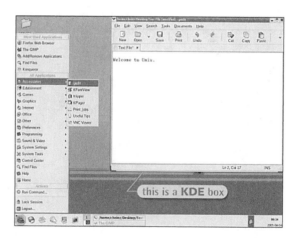

FIGURE 8.1   The KDE built-in editor.

The built-in KDE editor includes all the normal point-and-click selection, copying, insertion, and deletion features you might expect of a GUI-based editor. It is also cumbersome so be aware that when you want to use it, it may take a moment or two for it to load, especially if your system's hardware is not on the high end. When Microsoft Windows and Apple Macintosh users are waiting for an operation to complete (such as the loading of an application), they are at least given a warning that their system is being tied up. The KDE editor does not give you a warning, or an hourglass. You will need to be patient and wait for the editor to load. Don't assume your system is hung-up, nonresponsive, or ignoring you.

KDE will also allow you to navigate the file system by pointing your mouse and clicking on hyperlink-based icons. This is how you navigate your file system. To open a file to edit, you need only to select it. Choose a file to edit as seen in Figure 8.2.

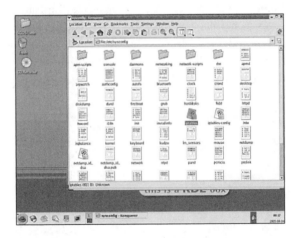

FIGURE 8.2   Finding a file to edit.

From here, you only need to edit your file. When you close the editing tool, you can save the file before you exit.

Summary

In this lesson, you were introduced to the two most popular text editors on the Unix platform: vi and emacs. Hopefully this chapter has motivated you to get a book on each one and delve deeper. Remember, editing files will be something you do often in the Unix environment, so it's important to know how to use at least one editor. In this lesson we introduced you to three of them; the `vi` editor, the `emacs` editor and the GUI-based editor. As long as you have the basics, you can grow from there.

Remember also that it is best to learn by doing, and this lesson provided you with the tools necessary to do the three most important tasks in a text editor:

- Starting the editor of your choosing

- Editing text

- Exiting and saving your work

Because you know how to quit both `vi` and `emacs` without saving, don't be afraid to experiment and make sure you spend some time on a practice system or practice lab working on these lessons until you have them mastered. Let's review before moving on to the next lesson, where we will learn about file-editing tools that add more functionality to your Unix skills toolkit.

- **`vi` editor**—This editor is fast and convenient for making small changes to files. It has a user interface that might be called non-intuitive at the kindest. The omnipresence of the `vi` editor, its speed of execution, and its small disk-space requirements make it a convenient choice for fast edits—and for when you're working at an unfamiliar machine.

- **Esc:**—This gets you out of `vi` in a hurry, without saving any changes you've made.

- **`emacs` editor**—The `emacs` editor contains everything you need in an editor, and then some, and then some more. On older hardware, `emacs` was very slow to start and respond, but today's fast machines and extremely inexpensive disk space and memory have largely mitigated this. Take the `emacs` tutorial, dig around in its info files, and find a book on `emacs` to read if you want to get the most out of this editor.

- **Ctrl+x Ctrl+c**—Followed by answering Yes to any "quit anyway?" questions, these keys get you out of `emacs` in a hurry, and without saving any changes you've made.

LESSON 9

Text and File Utilities

In this lesson we will learn about additional file editing and management utilities that can make your life easier in Unix.

In this section, we will wrap up file system management and editing. We have already covered the fundamentals of file creation and management; now we will look at some rare but helpful shell prompt commands that can really help you get some work done.

For example, when you create a book, there are many things that go into it. There is the typing, editing, and the file management and manipulation. For instance, to hand in a chapter that resembles a 10-minute lesson, the word count has to be set so that the reader can get through 8 to 10 pages of text in about 10 to 15 minutes. In a text file or word document, you will need to know the word count. Some of you may be familiar with how to go about getting your favorite word processing program to display this information.

In Unix, you can perform a word count with the wc command. In this chapter we will cover the wc command as well as other file management utilities to help you work efficiently in your Unix environment.

It's important to continue to move through each lesson in sequence as if you are a new learner, because you will see that certain commands can do different functions. For example, you may use a tool like grep in one lesson in a particular way, and then use it in a completely different way in a later lesson.

Using the information learned in this chapter in conjunction with other commands can be very powerful, just like Unix itself. If you take up shell scripting because of what you learned in Lesson 14, "Shell Scripting

Fundamentals," you will learn to love any tool or utility that can help you automate a job or function and make your life easier. Let's look at the wc command first.

The wc Command

In sum, the wc command counts words and provides you with a summary of what is found. Unix will report to you how many words are in a particular file. The wc stands for word count. When you want to see how many words are typed in a file, you simply need to execute the command and then the filename with its absolute or relative path. You will be shown the word count as well as the number of bytes, words, and lines in files.

The wc command is an excellent way to provide current statistics on a file you may want to work with. For example, if you wanted to issue the tail command on a file you think may be very large, you can use the wc command on a file to quickly see how many lines are in it. You can then use the tail command to jump the last grouping of text in the file you specify by line.

To use wc, simply supply the name of a file you want analyzed in the following form: **wc *<filename>*.** If you pass more than one filename to wc, all the files are processed, and a grand total for everything is returned. In the following example, we can see a simple query of a boot logfile that tells us what is picked up during Unix's inspection of the boot sequence when booting up.

```
>wc /var/log/boot.msg
340 225 20102 /var/log/boot.msg
```

This helps because I can see that the boot file is large and as I only wanted to see the end of it, I can now jump to the end using the tail command.

To read the command, you have to know what you are looking at. In this example, we saw a set of values returned by Unix when queried with the wc command. We see that the first value is 340. This is the number of lines in the file. The boot message file contains 340 lines. The second line is a count of the words in the file, and the third is the number of characters. The filename is just duplicated on the end of the line.

Is That a 250-Page Printout? Tree Killer In Lesson 17, "Printing with Unix," we will cover printing in detail. For now, you can use the wc command to see how large your print jobs are.

Now that we have learned about the wc command and how you can use it, what else is there to know? As mentioned earlier, this book is only large enough to skim the surface of what you can do. If you want to limit the values to lines, words, or characters, you can use the -l, -w, or -c options, respectively.

The `split` Command

Now that you know how to find out how much data is in a file, and what that file is comprised of logically to build up its internal structure, we will look at how to take a large file and break it down. The split command will do just that. It will cut down a file into whatever length you specify. To use the split command you need only to know that a file is too large to work with or to send to someone. Once this is determined, you can execute the split command to break it down. To split the file, take the following steps:

1. Choose your input file that you want to beak down. For example, I still have that boot log that is large, so I will break that down into manageable chunks.

2. Determine the number of lines you want stored in each output file. Understanding how to determine how many lines there are is important. This will help you determine what the sizing will be for the split. Do this by using -l <*number of lines*> as an option to the sort command.

output filename for the results.

using the following syntax: split <*segment
putfile*> <*outputfile*>.

An example of this functionality:

```
>split -l 3 boot.msg splitfile
```

The `boot.msg` file from the previous example has been run through `split` and has been divided into two files of three lines each. The `-l` option specified the 3 lines each. It's important to know this command if you want to break data down into manageable chunks so that you can either work with them or send them to others.

You may be wondering how you reassemble a file after you break and split it up. You can do this with a previously learned command, the `cat` command.

You need to reassemble your files that you just split. To do this, you need to use the `cat` command. When you have a series of files named with something such as *<name>* (*<name>*aa, *<basename>*ab, *<basename>*ac*<basename>*zz), you can reassemble them by issuing the `cat` command as follows: `cat` *<basename>*`* > combine_complete.file`. This will reassemble your files so that you can work with them.

Another handy set of utilities you will come to love is the `patch` and `diff` commands. These utilities will also help you with your Unix file management.

The `diff` and `patch` Commands

The `diff` and `patch` commands are a pair so we will cover them here together. Because of how they work, we will cover `diff` first.

When using `diff`, you will take two files, the original template file and an updated file that produces an output file. This file will contain enough information within it to be able to reconstruct the updated file when only given the patch file and template file. This can be handy if you want to only send out updates to, for example, a book, as you could send the edits instead of sending the entire file and replacing it. For smaller files this may not be a big deal, but for larger files that are of substantial size, and may have multiple people working on them, using `diff` may be very helpful to you.

To send out only the new material in a file, use the `diff` command with the following syntax: `diff <template file> <updated file> > <patchfile>`. The patchfile can be any filename you specify.

In this example, you can see how to create a patchfile.

```
>diff template.txt update.txt > patch.txt
```

The difference between the template file and the update file will be the patchfile. Try this command to see if it works for you in large file environments. If you can master this technique, it can save time creating, editing, and transferring files that you are collaborating on with others.

The `diff` command is also useful when you just want to know if two copies of the same file are identical or not. If you find yourself with multiple copies of similar files, `diff` is a fast and easy way to find out if they are identical. If the files are not identical, you will be able to see what changes have been made between them. No output produced by `diff` means that there are no differences between the files.

The `patch` command is also useful. It can be thought of as phase two of using the `diff` command. Now that you have your template, update, and new patchfile, you can use the `patch` with the file you want to fix. This can be seen as

```
>patch template.txt patch.txt
patching file 'template.txt'
```

The `patch` command will automatically update and patch the file named `template`. You applied the patch to the template and that was it. You can now use `cat` or `more` and view the files you created to see what the differences are between them. Always remember to keep a copy of your template file around. In this example, the patch was applied directly to the template file and the template file was updated. If all further patches are created from the updated file, no problem; however, if patches are created based on the original template, then the template.txt can no longer be patched.

Now you should be comfortable with most of the common Unix file management techniques such as learning how to create, read, edit, move, and copy files. You should also feel comfortable using fancy little tricks such as reading the head or tail of a file, or using grep for its contents. We have covered a lot about file management and you should be very proud of yourself if you nailed it. These 10-minute lessons are meant to show you the basics, get you moving, and expose you to the rest.

Tying It All Together: File Management Skills Test

Before we move on, I would like to take a moment to harp on the importance of Unix, the combination of commands to unleash the ultimate in power. This is what it's all about. Knowing commands will do nothing for you if you don't know how to use them from memory. In this section of the lesson, you will see what you remember and what you forgot, and how they (most of the Unix commands we have learned up to now) all work together when applied correctly.

In this example we will move through some of the commands that you have learned in the past nine lessons. This will not only serve as a refresher for you, but will also help you understand how they all can work together.

When working with files and directories, it is key to remember that the way Unix is organized is revolved around the files on your system and the directories in which they are contained. In this example, we will start by moving from your current directory into another one and create a file. Let's begin:

Skills Test

1. Most times, you will be working within your home directory. What would that look like at the shell prompt?

   Answer: ~

 Is There Another Name? In Unix, a home directory can also be called $HOME.

2. When you are working within the shell, it keeps track of the directory you are using. This directory is called the current working directory, or the current directory. To find your current directory, what would you type?

Answer: **pwd**

3. To list the files in the current directory, what would you type?

Answer: **ls**

What About Other Listings?   In Unix, you can use options with commands. This is especially true of the ls command.

With the ls command, you can do many switches, but a few options you should really keep in your personal memory banks are the following:

To list all the files in the current directory, including normally hidden files, type ls -a.

To list the files in the current directory and other additional information, such as the file's owner, its creation date, and its permissions, type ls -l.

To list the files in a directory, type ls <directory name>.

---

4. Now that you have listed the files in a directory, you may find that from the pwd and ls commands, you do not see the file you are looking for. You will see a directory within your present working directory that you know you want to work in; it's called storage. You need to change directories to storage where a file should be within it that we want to work on. To change the current directory to the storage directory, what would you type?

Answer: **cd storage**

Do I Always Need to Specify a Directory?   No, absolutely not. Specifying something is the easiest way to get right to it. If you do not know the name of the file, there is a handy tip you can learn to move quickly through the Unix file system until you reach the root directory, specified by a /.

To move up a directory, type `cd ...`

This will bring you to the directory just above the one you are currently in now. In other words, if you are in /etc, you will be in / if you issue the `cd ..` command. You must remember to leave a space, and the two dots.

You can also specify the direct path when you want to change a directory. You can be in the root directory and specify the path to the file you want by typing the entire path such as, `cd /etc/HTMLLAB/`. You can now edit a file within this path. In my example, it is indextest.htm.

5. From accessing the storage directory, we want to create a new directory where we can store only HTML files. You want to call the directory HTML. This being said, we need to create a new directory within the storage directory. To do this, what would you type?

Answer: `mkdir HTML`

Unix Is Sensitive Deep Down Inside   Remember, Unix is case sensitive. Although I made a directory in all uppercase letters, do not make the mistake of putting your caps lock key on. This is a big mistake in Unix environments, so break that habit quickly. Be careful when you use uppercase instead of lowercase; you could be specifying the wrong command.

6. You may have made a mistake and do not need this new directory. The `storage` directory should have contained a directory
   called `storage`. There are many ways for you to change this, but
   for this example we will look at using a tool to remove the
   unwanted directory, and create the new one when needed. To do
   this, what you would type?

   Answer: `rmdir HTML`

7. To create a new directory named `storage`, type `mkdir test`.
   When you complete this step, type `pwd` and `ls -l` to see what is
   in your current directory. Make sure you have the test directory
   created inside the directory you are currently located in. Once
   you ensure that this is good (you can walk back through the
   steps or the lessons in the book if you are having issues), your
   next step is to copy a file. You want to find a file in your current
   directory that you can copy to the test directory. If you are in
   your home directory, you may have a file in there to copy to
   another location. If you do not, then move to another directory
   (using the `cd` command) and search for a file to copy. You can
   run a generic search by issuing a wildcard such as **find /etc
   *.htm** or **find /etc *.conf** as examples. You will see Unix
   perform the search and then list out at the end all the files you
   requested. Once you find a file you want to copy, what would
   you type to copy that file to the `/etc/storage` directory?

   Answer: `cp syslog.conf /etc/storage`

   If you wanted to verify that this copied over, the follow-up to
   this command would be

   Answer: `ls -l /etc/storage`

   You should see that the file copied over. If not, check your work
   and go back through the steps just discussed.

 Unix Gone Wild   You can specify more than one file
with a path by using wildcards. A wildcard is a character that matches many characters. The * wildcard
matches any number of characters.

8. You have created a directory called storage and it currently has a file copied into it. You could have used the mv command to move it from its source directory to the destination, but that's not what we want. To remove a directory, you must first ensure that the directory does not contain any other files or directories using the rm command. You can then remove the storage directory by typing what?

Answer: **rmdir storage**

9. The last command I will show you is your reward for passing this small test. To prevent the servers from running out of disk space, your accounts are only allowed to store a limited amount of data. To find out how much room you have left, what command would you type at the shell prompt?

Answer: **quota**

This will give you the current disk quota for the current user.

Congratulations, you did a fantastic job in putting this all together. Imagine, you may not have even been working with Unix and now you have already mastered the basics. We haven't even scratched the surface of what Unix can do, and you are already navigating like a pro. Let's continue to the next lesson where we will wrap up file management by explaining to you how to manage your stored data through archiving and compression.

If you honestly had a very hard time working through this example, it is not because you can't do it, it is because you cannot recall the commands quickly. You should at least feel as if you *could* do it if you *had* those commands, right? Well, that's the trick to learning Unix; keep practicing, and practice makes perfect.

Summary

In this lesson we touched on some of the more obscure and specialized file management commands contained within Unix's command-line toolkit. Commands such as wc and split can help you perform word counts, break up your files, and reassemble your files. You learned of `diff` and `split`, which are used to help you do file size comparisons and updates with ease. Lastly, we spent some time working through a small exercise meant to show you how to use file management commands in sequence. We also reviewed most (if not all) the basic file management commands and how they can work together. Review the lessons and make up your own tests and drills and you will be a Unix pro in no time! Here's a review of what was learned in this lesson:

- **wc**—The wc command can provide quick character, line, and word counts for a single file or for a group of files.

- **split**—If you have files that are a bit too large to handle when sending email, writing to a floppy, and so on, you can use the split command to chop them up into smaller files. split can create files containing a certain number of lines, kilobytes, or megabytes.

- **diff/patch**—The combination of diff and patch enables you to distribute updates (to documents, source code, and so on) in an efficient manner. Rather than sending copies of entire updated files, you can use diff to create patchfiles that only contain the changes between one version of a file and the next.

- **File Management Skill Review**—The combination of all the file management commands you learned is essentially where the power of Unix comes from; the batch automation of many commands added together is how Unix can do anything scripted. It's important to master this idea now, and keep working on it, so that as you progress with Unix, you can combine many cryptic commands at will.

LESSON 10

Compression and Archiving Tools

In this lesson, you will learn about common Unix tools for compressing and archiving files, as well as a few tools you can use to keep tabs on your disk usage.

Managing Files in Unix

When you send files across the Internet through email, update your website, store files on a home-based intranet, or play movies on your computer, you are working with data that takes up space on your system. Regardless of what system, Microsoft Windows, Apple Macintosh, Unix, or Linux, you will need to have a spot to keep all this information you want to store.

This data is kept in storage space in the form of hard disks where your Unix system is most likely installed and where your data probably resides. Hard disks are commonly filled up and close to capacity in most cases. It always seems like you need more space—although over the years the amount of space that you can purchase seems incredibly high, most folks still pile on the data. However, there is no need to worry. That's why almost every operating system created comes with some form of archiving and compression utility. There are third party tools galore to perform this function as well. You may even find compression and archiving tools in your email client as well!

There are other reasons for knowing how to manage files in Unix when considering archiving and compression. For example, when you get updates, or need to install software on your Unix system, most likely you will receive this update in a compressed or archived manner and you will need to know how to utilize tools like tar. The tar tool allows you to install things on your Unix system. This is common if you are a systems administrator. As a Unix end user, you may not need to install anything but this is good to know regardless.

In this chapter, we will cover the Unix compression and archiving tools that you will need to use or become familiar with as Unix users. Before we move on, let's quickly review some of the commands you will need to know.

Managing Your Disk Usage

If you're on a system where you need to worry about disk usage, have a disk quota (we learned about this in the last lesson) that you must remain under, or are just curious about how much space your files are taking up, there are a number of ways for you to look at this data. These commands are detailed in the following list:

- **ls**—Referring back to Lesson 4, "The File System Explained," you know that you can use the ls command with the -l option to display disk usage for a file or files. If you need to scan quickly through your files to see which ones are taking up the most space, this is a quick way to do it.

- **find**—In Lesson 5, "File System Navigation Techniques," you were introduced to using the find command to find files larger than a certain size. Although similar in utility to the ls -l command for this purpose, find -size # is a faster way to collect information on all files larger than # kilobytes. You just need to know what # you're looking for.

- **df**—Used mostly by system administrators, the df command gives information about disk usage. Depending on your version of Unix, you might have to give df different options to get it to produce readable output; but the general form you'd be interested in is df ./, which asks the file system to tell you about the usage of the drive upon which the current directory resides. The response is usually in the form of a logical device name (which you can ignore), followed by information about the total capacity of the device, the amount of storage in use on the device, the percentage of usage of the device, and the *mount point* (path to the directory at which the device appears) for the device. You might have to try variations on df ./ or df -k ./, or check your man pages to find the option that works on your version of Unix.

- **du**—Another command for system administrators, du provides information about disk usage by directory. Again, different versions of Unix use slightly different syntaxes; the general form you will be most interested in is du -s *, which asks the file system to produce a disk usage summary for everything in the current directory. For each item in the current directory, du -s * returns a summary of the total disk space used by the contents of the files or directories. Depending on your version of Unix, you might need to supply du with the -k flag to convince it to show you the disk usage in values of kilobytes (otherwise it shows you the disk usage in values of the file system's native block size, usually 512 bytes).

Wrap this into the other commands you have learned and you will know exactly how to see what is on your hard disk, what space it's taking up, and what you can do with that data to increase space (move it, delete it, archive it, and so on).

 Master Your Commands   As I have harped in previous chapters, you must continue to recall the commands you previously learned. Keep the commands fresh in your mind and keep practicing. Commands like ls will be used constantly as you work with Unix.

Compressing Files in Unix

The sole reason for compressing files is to save space. You want to save space, so you make room. This is analogous to closet space in your home. Often, you can buy something that will allow you to organize and condense your space so that you have more room to put more things in. This theoretically is the same concept behind compression. You take something, squeeze it down, and organize it so that you can store more.

You can also compress files to send them to others. This is common with digital photography and today's email clients. Many people have email and digital cameras, and they want to send photos through email. Often an email of this size will be denied because the person you are sending it to may not have enough space on her system, or in the mailbox on the email server, to accept a file that size. Therefore, you will need to compress it.

Makes sense, right? Well, that's all you need to know about why to compress something. Now you need to know the actual mechanics of it.

If you happen to be using a system where disk space is restricted and you need to maximize available space, you can use the Unix commands you will learn here. These commands will reduce the amount of space your files occupy, and will allow you to store more files in the space you are allowed.

There are three major compression formats you will use when working with Unix:

- Unix program `compress` makes *compressed* files

- Personal or third party Unix programs (such as `PKZIP` program) make *zipped* files

- Unix GNU program `gzip` makes *gzipped* files

We will cover all of these in both compressing and decompressing (or uncompressing) formats, as you will need to know how to decompress something that you compressed. Each of these formats has a set of programs for compressing and uncompressing. For our first example, we shall look at the standard (and hardly used) compress tool that comes with almost every distribution of Unix.

Why Compress? By applying an algorithm, you can compress files for the purpose of conserving space or speeding up file transfers.

The `compress` Command

Use this command and specify what you want to compress. The `compress` command, when used, will be seen as `compress <filename>`. The `compress` command is an older Unix command that uses an older algorithm to make the compression. In fact, this tool is not commonly used anymore, but it does exist on just about every version of Unix. Better compression algorithms have since been developed; that's why it's been moved to the side and replaced by tools such as `gzip`.

Files created with the `compress` command have the file suffix `.Z`. This will appear in the directory in which you compressed the original file, and can be seen by using the `ls -l` command.

The `uncompress` command uncompresses the results of a `compress` command. To use the `uncompress` command, you issue the command as `uncompress <filename.Z>`.

Remember learning about how the `cat` command can be used to read files? The `zcat` command is a version of `cat` that reads compressed files rather than normal text files. Using `zcat` is similar to using `compress` and `uncompress`; issue the command as `zcat <filename.Z>`. Remember, since you already compressed a file, the file suffix is `.Z`.

May the GNU Be with You It's common to use compression utilities if you are trying to save space. Don't get too hung up on using `compress`; instead consider using `gzip`.

The `gzip` Command

Using the compress command will get you the results you need, but again, the utility is older and does not work as well as newer ones. Also, the

Unix version of compress can be slightly altered as you go from distribution to distribution. Any variance is not good as you may not be able to compress with one utility and decompress with another. To make this point clearer, consider why you would use compress: because it is the only thing you either know or have. It is located on your local Unix system and is there for use.

What if you wanted to use something that was a little less likely to be proprietary? The gzip command (stands for GNU zip) is the original file compression program for GNU/Linux and has been adopted for use with all Unix systems under the GPL (GNU Public License). This means that it is free for use and standardized as a common tool that almost everyone in Unix and Linux environments will use. Current versions of gzip produce files with a .gz extension.

The gzip command will work essentially identically to the compress/uncompress/zcat suite we just talked about. It is a better utility and less proprietary than the older tools in use such as compress.

To make your life a bit easier, GNU has included the capability to deal with compressed (.Z) files in their gunzip and gzcat utilities. You might find that gzip and gunzip exist on your system, but that gzcat is missing. Some distributions have renamed gzcat to zcat because it handles compressed files as well.

When gzip is combined with tar (which stands for Tape Archive and will be discussed later), the resulting file extensions may be .tgz, .tar.gz, or tar.Z.

zip/unzip

As we wind down to the end of our compression utilities offerings that can be used with Unix, let's cover the last of the commonly seen utilities used for compression and decompression. Most PC users, whether familiar with Unix or not, know about Zip files. The zip command offers compression that is based on the algorithm from the PC standard PKZip program. The zip and unzip programs work exactly as you might expect them to: **zip** *<filename>* to compress a file with zip, and **unzip** *<filename.z>* to unzip the files.

What Can `bzip2` Do for You?   Also appearing recently is the `bzip2` compression utility, which despite being the newer kid on the block, looks very promising for tight compression. You can learn more about this tool at the bzip website at http://www.bzip.org/.

`bzip2` is a freely available, high-quality data compressor. The current version is 1.0.3, released February 15, 2005, so it's still being updated as of the writing of this book.

It typically compresses files to within 10% to 15% of the best available techniques, while still being around twice as fast at compression and six times faster at decompression. This being said, it would make sense that if you need to have this higher rate of compression, you should use this utility. Many users still faithfully use `gzip`.

The syntax and options for `bzip2` have intentionally been made similar to `gzip`, so if you encounter this program as it grows in popularity, you won't have too much trouble figuring it out. Compression with `bzip2` follows the `gzip` format **`bzip2 <filename>`**, which produces the compressed file <filename.bz2>. Decompression is simply **`bunzip2 <filename.bz2>`**.

Since this utility is not common to see or use, if you encounter `bzip2` and need to do more than trivial compressions or decompressions, it is recommended that you consult your local man pages for more current information.

Creating files using the `zip` format (which uses the file suffix `.z` in Unix) for distribution to other Unix users is generally not a good idea, as `zip` and `unzip` are not always available to Unix users. These utilities are freeware, so get your system administrator to install them if you need to have access to them.

If your target, however, is users of Macintosh or Windows computers, zip is a file format that they can most likely read. Both the zip and unzip programs have a number of potentially useful options, a list of which can be displayed by issuing either command followed by the option -h.

In this section of the lesson, we have covered how to compress data, and we lightly touched on the use of the tar command. In the next section, we will dig deeper into the tar command and cover its use.

The tar Command

If you spend much time using Unix systems, you're bound to run into tar files. The tar command is a convenient and commonly used tool for personal archiving and distribution of files. It's imperative that you are familiar with tar if you are going to study Unix beyond the level of this book. As mentioned before, *tar* stands for Tape Archive, although this is used more often for standard packaging. It was originally designed for tape backup, but today can be used with other storage media.

What is packaging? Well, let's say you needed to send someone a program you created. You would most likely not just have one file, but multiple files. You may want to create a single file that basically encompasses all the rest of the files or directories you are looking to package. The purpose of assembling a collection of files into one combined file is for easier archiving, storage, and sending condensed versions of data to others. When run by itself, it produces files with a .tar extension. When combined with gzip, for data compression, the resulting file extensions may be .tgz, .tar.gz, or .tar.Z as mentioned earlier.

The tar command in its simplest form either creates or unpacks archive files. When creating an archive, you provide tar with a filename for the archive and a list of files that you want to archive. The tar program will collect all the files you specify and put them into one single file—this is commonly called a *tarball*.

When unpacking archives, you provide tar with the name of a tar file and it extracts the contents of the file into the current directory, or a directory you specify with the exact same filenames, paths, and contents that existed on the system where it was tarred.

To use `tar` to create an archive, use the following steps:

1. Select the data you want to archive and develop a name for the `tar` file itself. For example, since it's an archive, you may want to use dates along with an appropriate title so that you can see what kind of archive it is. This is not mandatory of course, just a suggestion.

2. Issue the `tar` command as `tar -cvf <tarfilename.tar> <files or directories>`.

To picture this in use, consider having a directory named `storage` and you want to archive it. Everything in `storage` will be contained in the `tar` file that is created.

```
> tar -cvf storage030105.tar storage
```

In this example, I took the `storage` directory and made a `tar` file out of it called `storage030105.tar`. I used a date method so that I could keep track of what I was saving and when I saved it. In this example, we also see options being used (such as `-cvf`), so let's cover what you can do with the `tar` command and its options.

There are many options you can use with the `tar` command. If you type **tar --help**, you will be amazed at how much you can do with the `tar` command. In this example, we used the `-cvf` options.

The `-c` option specifies to Unix that your intentions are on creating a new archive. The `-v` (or verbose) option will show you all the files that are being packaged. The `-f` option tells Unix whether to put this data in a file archive.

This new file contains the entire contents of your `storage` directory with all the directory structure and file attribute information intact. To unpack a `tar` file, you simply issue the command `tar -xvf <tarfilename.tar>`.

In this example, all the options are the same except for one. The `-x` option is used here when *extracting* your files from the `tar` archive. This can be seen here:

```
> tar -xvf storage030105.tar
```

After a list of everything in the file is shown by the verbose option, you will have extracted this file (and all its contents) identically into the current directory you are in now. Sometimes you may want to view what is in a tar file before you extract it. You can do this by changing the options. Type **tar -tvf <*tarfile.tar*>** before unpacking it if you are not sure what may be in a file you are ready to extract. The -t option is the *list* option, and asks tar to tell you about the contents of the file rather than unpack it. This is helpful if you want to quickly see what is inside.

Using uuencode/uudecode

To send your files to another person either through a tool such as FTP (stands for File Transfer Protocol and efficiently transfers files from a source to a destination) or through email, you may need to adjust things. For instance, you may need to send an email to a Macintosh user that uses Binhex. This is just another encoding scheme. Because of this, you may have to change the specification of the data you send in your email attachment. This is not common for users who are accustomed to using Windows, although email within Windows also uses uuencode. Long story short, it is imperative as a Unix user that you know how to adjust this because you may have to specify it with Unix.

Uuen-what?   Uuencode stands for a set of algorithms for converting files into a series of 7-bit ASCII charac-ters that can be transmitted over the Internet. Originally, uuencode stood for Unix-to-Unix encode, but it has since become a universal protocol used to transfer files between different platforms such as Unix, Windows, and Macintosh. Uuencoding is especially popular for sending email attachments. Nearly all email applications support uuencoding for sending attachments and uudecoding for receiving attachments.

The uuencode program accepts any file as input, and it produces an encoding of the file that can be included in an email message. To a person, the contents of this file look like random characters; on the receiving end, however, the user can use the uudecode command to extract the original file. Let's look at how that would work:

To use the uuencode command, you need to follow these steps:

1. Select a file you want to email.

2. Issue the uuencode command as uuencode *<filename>* *<callmethis>* > *<filename>*.uue. (You need to type the > before the *<filename>*.uue argument.)

Your computer will then produce a file named <filename>.uue, which contains the uuencoded version of the file. For example, if you have a file named test and you want to uuencode it, you can type the following:

> **uuencode testsend > testsent test.uue**

Your computer produces a file named test.uue, which when decoded will be named testsent and contains the contents of your testsend file. Now you can copy and paste, or do whatever you need to do to insert the file you just created into an email message and send it wherever you want.

Of course, if you receive a uuencoded file, you need to know how to decode the file. Decoding a uuencoded file is also extremely simple; issue the uudecode command as uudecode *<filename.uue>*. Your machine will produce a file in the current directory identical to the one originally uuencoded.

Summary

In this lesson we covered how to archive and compress files and other data on your Unix system. This wraps up the file management portion of this book. In our next lesson, we will start to learn more about your shell, and in particular, the processes running on your Unix system. Here's a look at what was learned in this lesson:

- The three common compression utilities on Unix systems are the omnipresent compress, the newer and smarter gzip, and the cross-platform zip programs. A relatively new addition to the Unix compression scene is bzip2, which appears to produce better compression than compress or gzip.

- When you need to provide a collection of files to other users, or simply archive a set of files for future use, you can use tar to create tar files that contain all your files in one convenient package.

- If you need to send a file to someone through email, you can create an email-able encoding of the file by using the uuencode command.

- Don't be alarmed if you uudecode a file and can't immediately find it. The real filename is stored in plain text at the beginning of the file.

LESSON 11

Managing Processes in Unix

In this lesson, you will learn how to work with Unix's internal processes.

In this lesson, we will continue to unleash the power of Unix by learning to work with processes. All the tools we have worked with in the first 10 lessons create processes on your Unix system. In other words, if you use a command that starts an email client on your Unix system (such as `sendmail`), you have started an internal process within Unix that runs to support the email client. Each command used in Unix creates a process that the Unix operating system runs until it is finished or *killed*. The word *kill* refers to ending a process in Unix.

What Is a Process? In the dictionary, the term *process* can be defined as a procedure or a particular course of action intended to achieve a desired result.

In computer terminology (namely, in your Unix environment), a process is a single executable module (also known as a *code* or *program*) that runs concurrently with other executable modules.

Unix is flexible. You can create processes that run entirely in the background or that start and run in the middle of the night without needing you to be logged into the computer. In this lesson, we will learn how to use Unix to start and stop processes. We will also learn commands that help automate processes. Automation means that you do not have to manually input a command; it can be done automatically by a tool (such as `at`) to help ease your workload.

Multitasking

In this section, we will cover what is known as multitasking and how it works with Unix. Multitasking is the capability of a CPU (central processing unit), which is the brain of your Unix system, to handle more than one operation at a time. For instance, the capability to run a word processing tool and an email client at the same time without crashing your computer would be considered multitasking. Unix allows you to multitask in that it lets you run more than one process at a time. Remember, with Unix, every command or program that you use is considered a process.

Background Processes

Many times you will want something to run on your Unix system but you won't want to see or use it while it is running. Having this process in the foreground will only cause you to waste time watching something that could be taking place without your input. In this situation, you would want to run a background process. Whereas a foreground process remains in the foreground and usually takes up many of the resources available on your system, a background process can run largely without your intervention.

Making a command run in the background is simple; you simply add an ampersand (&) to the end of the line containing the command. For example, you could use & to run the cron or at commands in the background. The cron command is used for scheduling jobs to be executed regularly after a designated period of time. The at command is for executing commands once at a single specified time. These commands will be discussed in greater depth later in the lesson.

Using Ctrl+z and bg

In Unix, you can stop any process that is running by pressing **Ctrl+z**. Suspending a command and moving it to the background is another story. do this, you must be familiar with **Ctrl+z** as well as and: the bg command.

To turn any process into a background process, first press **Ctrl+z** to suspend the process if it is running and you did not enter an ampersand following the command. Consider the following example:

```
Ctrl+z
[10]+  Stopped                 at 2
```

Here, the at command has been suspended and assigned job number 10.

The process ID (PID) (as shown with the ps command) is a number used by the kernel to keep track of every process running on the system. This is not the same as the job number. The job number will identify the process number locally in your session, not globally to the system.

PID Versus Job   Every process running on a Unix system is assigned a unique PID. Every process you start is also assigned a job number. The job number is only unique to your current session. If you open a Terminal window and start a command, the first command will often get the job number 1. If you open a different Terminal and start another process in that, that process may also get the job number 1. Using the job number in either terminal will only affect the process started in that terminal. Thus PIDs are used globally across the entire system to keep track of processes, whereas job numbers local to the specific session in which they where started.

To move the suspended process to the background, you only need to use the bg command and add the job number directly behind it. In the case of our example, the command would look like this:

```
>bg %10
```

As you can see, the background command is easy to use and helpful if you want to run multiple jobs while still being able to control and work with Unix.

The `fg` Command

Just as you can send processes to the background, you can also bring
them back to the foreground. This is done by using the foreground (`fg`)
command. Let's return to our example. If you wanted to bring the `at`
command back to the foreground, you would simply enter the following:

```
>fg %10
```

With the `fg` command, you can quickly bring the process you want to
work on to the foreground. When you are done working with this process,
you can send it back again with the `bg` command.

The `jobs` Command

When working in Unix, it is easy to forget what local processes are
running. Say you need to bring a background process to the foreground
but you don't know the job number you need to select. Here, the `jobs`
command will show you what the job number is if you have forgotten it.
Simply type **jobs** at the shell prompt and you will be shown the ID
numbers for any processes you have started or stopped.

```
> jobs
```

The `jobs` command will also provide you with a history of sorts; using
this command will list all previous process that have been started and
stopped.

We now come to one of the most important commands in this lesson: the
`ps` command.

The `ps` Command

The `ps` command will list your current processes. You can also run
processes with this command. The `ps` command is helpful because once
you start using the background capabilities of Unix, at some point you
will need to find out what all you have running. After all, if you continue

to aimlessly start process after process, you may find that you have a lot more running on your Unix system than you want. In Unix, you can run the ps command at the shell prompt. Once you do this, you will see something similar to the following:

```
>ps
  PID TTY STAT   TIME COMMAND
 8832  p1 R     0:00 ps
30675  p1 S     0:00 -bash
(Output removed)
```

If you run ps and see this result, you are looking at a list of all the commands you currently have running. Don't be alarmed if you do not see the same output as that listed here; the ps command generates slightly different results in different versions of Unix and Linux. Nonetheless, the same information is generally provided in each version.

How, then, do you interpret this output? From left to right, the columns indicate the system process ID (PID), the controlling terminal, the status of the process (running, sleeping, and so on), and the process itself. Some versions won't show you the status, but this varies depending on what Unix distro you are using. In most cases, however, typing the ps command will provide you with the most important things you need to know, which are the PID and the processes in use.

Where Are the Processes? In our example, we saw only a couple of processes running. Could those really be all the processes? There aren't any more than that? There have to be, right?

Yes, there are other processes running, and to see them all, you have to know the proper option for the ps command. If you just enter **ps**, you will see a list of all the processes you own, but to see a listing of the processes owned by all users, you need to enter either **ps -ax** or **ps -ef**.

In addition to understanding the ps command, you should also understand how to stop or kill a process.

The kill Command

When you use the kill command with a process, you stop whatever that process is doing. One hazard with commands of this nature is that if you are using a program like the vi editor and you kill it, you may lose your work as a result.

Although the kill command is mainly used to end a process, it can also be used to send signals to a process. Signals can be sent to indicate an action. There are actually many signals that you can use with the kill command. If you use the kill command with the -1 option, you can see a list of everything that Unix can signal with:

```
>kill -1
 1) SIGHUP      2) SIGINT      3) SIGQUIT     4) SIGILL
 5) SIGTRAP     6) SIGIOT      7) SIGBUS      8) SIGFPE
 9) SIGKILL    10) SIGUSR1    11) SIGSEGV    12) SIGUSR2
13) SIGPIPE    14) SIGALRM    15) SIGTERM    17) SIGCHLD
18) SIGCONT    19) SIGSTOP    20) SIGTSTP    21) SIGTTIN
22) SIGTTOU    23) SIGURG     24) SIGXCPU    25) SIGXFSZ
26) SIGVTALRM  27) SIGPROF    28) SIGWINCH   29) SIGIO
30) SIGPWR
```

Documentation for the software you run on your system often includes information on the signals to which it will respond. The most important signals you'll use are SIGHUP and SIGKILL. The SIGHUP signal will hang up and reload the server's process configuration information. SIGKILL should be pretty self-explanatory; KILL in all capital letters should help you remember that this is the signal to kill processes. To use the kill command, enter **kill -<signal number> <process ID> <process ID> ....**

For example, to kill process number 8832, type the following:

```
>kill -9 8832
```

If you look at the process listing again, PID 8832 will be gone. You've
successfully killed it! Check by verifying with the ps command and make
sure that the process has ended. You can also check with the jobs
command as well.

> **Getting on Top**   The top command can be used to
> quickly identify running processes, and it continuously
> updates a list of them for you to view. It's really a
> great command when you want to know what your
> Unix system is doing. The top command can also help
> you see the amount of time being used by each
> process and the processes' priority.
>
> To exit out of top, press **Ctrl+c** or **q**.

So now that you are comfortable working with commands such as top,
jobs, ps, and kill, let's look at some of the other commands you will
need to know to control processes within Unix, namely cron and at.

The at and cron Commands

Thus far we have only touched on commands that will allow you to automate processes, because automation is the easiest way to get things done.
If you know how to automate something, then it's as simple as setting up
the job one time and having it run on a schedule. In this section of the
lesson, we will talk about how the at and cron commands can help you
automate tasks in Unix. There is a great deal to talk about when considering backups and running complex processes with these commands, and
we cannot dig into these topics in-depth in a book of this nature. For now,
be aware that these commands are powerful and there is much more to
learn about them. You may want to dig into this subject a bit deeper if you
continue to work with Unix.

So, when considering backups in particular but any process overall, Unix
users may need to schedule jobs with the at and cron commands. Let's
look at how this can be done.

Hey You—Back Up! Backups are a part of life when you want to make sure that your data (files and directories) are recoverable in case you delete something or make a mistake.

Unix is not forgiving, so if you do make a mistake, your only recourse is to get a copy of the missing or deleted data. You would get this copy from a backup source, most likely a tape backup system if you are at work. If you are at home, just about any media device can be used for backup. Remember, backups are important, because if you ever need a copy of your data, backups ensure that the copy is there.

There are two basic ways to set up your Unix system to run a command (process) at a specific time; one way is to use the cron command, and the other is to use the at command. Your Unix system will most likely always have the cron process running, but in many cases, if this command is not needed, it will be disabled by your Unix system administrator. (For security reasons, it is common in most environments to always terminate, disable, and remove anything from a system that its users don't need to do their work. If you are running Unix at home for fun, then you may have just about everything running on your system if you are logged in as root or a SuperUser.) In any case, cron (if enabled) will allow you to automate complex jobs such as log rotations, backups, cleanup commands, and so on. The cron command will do this on a continuous schedule that you configure. cron enables you to run commands in intervals as small as one second or as long as one year.

You should also know what a crontab is, because this term will most certainly come up when you work with a Unix- or Linux-based operating system. You can create a personal crontab file that holds information about the interval on which you want a command to run. You can then use the crontab <filename> command to add your request to the system's crontab file. With some Unix versions, you can use crontab -e to bring up your currently set crontab entries directly into an editor as well.

Using cron

As mentioned earlier in the lesson, the cron process (also called the cron daemon) executes commands at specific dates and times. You can use cron to schedule activities, either as one-time events or as recurring tasks. Remember, if you want to attempt to work with cron, you may have to request to do so. On most systems, you must get permission from the system administrator before you can submit job requests to cron. Similarly, on some shared systems, because there is only one crontab file, only the administrator has access to the crontab command.

As mentioned earlier, for commands that need to be executed repeatedly (for example, hourly, daily, or weekly), you can use the crontab command. The crontab command creates a crontab file containing commands and instructions for the cron daemon to execute. You can use the crontab command with many options. If you can master this command, you can automate almost any process for any reason. Let's look at crontab at work.

To use crontab, simple type **crontab** with an option and then the filename. The filename that you specify will be used for your crontab file. Many times, you can just leave out the option and simply type **crontab filename** to save that file as your crontab file. An example would be

```
>crontab -a filename
```

The -a option (again, not always needed on some Unix variations) will install the filename as your crontab file. You can also use other options, such as crontab -e. This will allow you to edit your crontab file; obviously, if you want to change processes, then this is important to know about and be able to do. You can display your crontab file with the -1 option. You can use -r to remove your crontab file. There are more options for crontab (consult your man pages for additional information), but they are more complex and used for system administration. This overview should be enough to get you started with local automation on your Unix system.

Each entry in a crontab file consists of six fields, specifying (in order) the following information:

```
minute(s) hour(s) day(s) month(s) weekday(s) command(s)
```

The six fields are separated from one another by spaces or tabs. The first five fields are integer patterns, and the sixth is the command to be executed. Each field is pretty self-explanatory as to what information it requires; the command field obviously names the process itself or the complete sequence of commands to execute. This can also be a shell script. We will cover shell scripts in Lesson 14, "Shell Scripting Fundamentals."

Be Careful with cron—If you want to use cron, crontab, or at, it is highly recommended that you check with your Unix system administrator if the system you are working with is not your own. Scheduling processes blindly can affect other users of the system (remember, Unix can serve many people at once), and if you run too many processes or schedule something incorrectly, you may cause problems to your system that will affect not only you but everyone else who uses the system.

You may or may not be alerted if your cron, crontab, or at command creates any problems. If a cron job specified in your crontab entry produces any error messages when it runs, you will get a mail message reporting the errors.

Using at

The at command enables you to run a command once rather than at a repeating interval like cron does. This is useful if there is a processor-intensive task that you want to run after business hours so that other tasks aren't affected.

To schedule a one-time-only task use the at or batch command. To submit a job with the at command, you only need to enter the at command itself and the runtime you want, which is simply the date and time you want the job (process) to execute:

```
> at runtime
```

Pressing enter here, however, doesn't do anything but enter you into a new mode with a new prompt, most likely resembling the following:

```
at>
```

What you will see varies among different distributions of Unix, but most times, this is exactly what will appear on your console. At this secondary prompt, you need to just enter the command you would like to run. You can check the status of your command at the system console.

Two Unix Commands for the Price of One!   The batch command is similar to at. The syntax for batch is identical to at, except that you do not set an execution time.

So, now that we know how to open it up and get it ready, let's look at the at command in action.

```
> at noon
at>tar -cf /users/rob/storage storage.tar
at>Ctrl-d
```

In this example, the user submitted a job that will run at noon the same day if submitted in the morning, or noon the next day if submitted in the afternoon. As well, at will create a tarball of /users/rob/storage directory and call it storage.tar. You can use **Ctrl+d** to break out of the at process and return to your shell prompt.

Who's the Man?   There is a lot more to learn about all the commands we have covered. Continue to use your man pages as often as you can and keep your memorization of these commands to a premium level if you want speed and accuracy every time you come to the console. Unix is intimidating, but as you can see, it's not hard to use and to learn about. Continue to check the man pages when you need help. Some helpful man pages related to the content of this lesson include man crontab, man cron, man at, and man batch.

Summary

We've covered a lot of ground in this lesson, but at the same time, we've only scratched the surface. Unfortunately, there is too much to know about cron and at to fit into this 10-minute lesson. For more information, consult your local man pages. Understanding processes can be a bit difficult at first, but depending on your use of the system, you might never need to do much more than put a process into the background. If you use KDE exclusively, you'll find that processes work exactly as you might expect on any desktop operating system. In addition, you can easily open a shell prompt and use all of these commands and reference their man pages. You can also use your current X Window System help system.

The following is a quick review of what was discussed in this lesson:

- **&**—The ampersand can be used to put a process into the background. Use this if you are running something that takes a long time to complete and that requires little or no user interaction.

- **bg/fg**—The bg and fg commands can be used to move processes to and from background or foreground operation.

- **ps**—To list all the processes that you are running on your system, use the ps command. You can also view processes that are controlled by other users, but you can't modify their priority or kill them.

- **kill**—This command is used to send a signal to a process. Normally, this signal terminates the execution of the process. In other cases, it can cause a program to reread its configuration file or reinitialize itself.

- **nohup**—Exiting a shell sends a SIGHUP (hangup) signal to all the running processes in that shell. To enable a process to continue running even after you log off, use the nohup command.

- **nice/renice**—Every process on the computer has a priority that controls how much processor time a process gets in order to complete its task. Priorities range from -20 to 20, with the negative numbers being the higher priority.

- **top**—The top command shows the amount of CPU time being used by the processes that are currently running on your system. The display continuously updates, so you can view how much CPU time new processes take as they are added to the system.

- **at/crontab**—You can schedule commands to run at certain times on your system by using the at and crontab functions. You will want to check with your system administrator and read the appropriate man pages before attempting to do so.

LESSON 12

Input and Output

In this lesson, you will learn how to manage Unix processes. We will cover input and output and how it relates to Unix.

We have learned a great deal about the Unix operating system itself. We have covered Unix tools that when opened and executed with commands become running processes (or daemons) on your Unix machine. In this lesson, we will cover the fundamentals of input and output and how it relates to Unix.

We have discussed the file system, as well as what processes are and how to manage them. We will now cover interprocess communication by input and output redirection and show you some of the underlying power Unix holds within. Unix is powerful and learning how to manage input and output (or I/O for short) is at the center of unleashing that power. Unix considers user input and program output back to the user as a stream. This is commonly referred to as a stream of information. This is how the concept of redirection is built. Redirection is when you specify to a program to send its part of the stream (output) to somewhere else other than the default (back to the user).

The purpose of this lesson is to introduce you to some features of I/O in an operating system, and how you can practice them to build your skills up. This 10-minute lesson is built to open your eyes to input and output management. However, it is up to you to dig deeper and learn more about it. A good source of information is the man pages.

I/O Redirection

With Unix, I/O redirection is defined as nothing more than sending input or output to somewhere other than the default locations, specifying a different or alternative destination. Input and output redirection is done with special characters.

It should be noted that every Unix shell offers I/O redirection with a standard set of characters used to achieve it. Those characters are

<, which redirects standard input to come from a file

>, which redirects standard output to go to a file

There are other characters that we will learn about, but for now, these are the two most common forms of I/O redirection known or used.

We will look at an example of using these characters with the `cat` command. We learned about this command when we learned how to read files in Unix.

The `cat` command is actually short for *concatenate*. Concatenate means "to link together" and is the perfect definition for the examples I am about to show you. The `cat` command will allow you to specify multiple filename arguments, and then `cat` will copy them to standard output, better known as STDOUT. We will cover this shortly. When using `cat`, remember that we used the `'command < filename'` syntax here. This means that you want to change what was standard output for `cat` and change it to what you specify. Simple, right? If standard behavior for running `cat` without any arguments is to just repeat any input back to the terminal, then `cat > filename` can change how I/O is directed so that in this case all the input will be directed into the file.

```
>cat
1
1
2
2
Crtl+d
```

In this example, we showed that the `cat` command, when used without a filename argument, simply copies its current input to its output. This is why when you typed 1, `cat` was nice enough to repeat it back to you. This proves a point about input and output. You invoked the `cat` command, it waited for your input, and then repeated it as output. This should solidify what I/O really is within Unix at its most fundamental level.

To show how redirection works, let's take the `cat` command one step further. We covered the usage of both the characters; now let's see them in action. We already learned how to copy a file from one location to another with the `cp` command; now we will learn how to do it through redirection with `cat`.

```
> cat  < testfile1  >  testfile2
```

The concepts of I/O, redirection, and the usage of special characters should start to make more sense from these simple examples. One last note to be mentioned is that input and output redirectors can be combined. We saw this in the last example where we used the first character to change its input, and then the second character defined the output. Both the standard input STDIN and output STDOUT were changed from their defaults. Both of these terms will be covered next.

Standard I/O

Now that you understand what I/O is, and how commands in Unix work with redirection, it's time to cover what standard input and output is, as well as standard error. In this section of the lesson, we will cover how Unix accepts input and output and errors by default.

When each Unix program is created, it will have a way to accept input. Unix itself is not only based on I/O, but so is every program that runs within it. Unix, when operated through the shell prompt, allows you to control I/O completely, which is why such characters can be used in shell scripts, which will be covered in Lesson 14, "Shell Scripting Fundamentals." In the last lesson we learned how to use `cron` to automate, and it could automate a script. Think of the shell prompt commands and processes we have learned. It should be clear to you that if you master what we have learned, and shell scripting, the power of Unix dwarfs its competitors. Unix is flexible in just about every way imaginable. One of the things you can do with I/O management is redirect input from any standard location to anything you specify.

As mentioned, you can redirect input and output to come from or go to a file, but that is not the only way I/O can be used. You can also send the contents of a file to someone as an email. It is virtually limitless as to what you can do when learning how to manage I/O; the secret is in learning the commands and characters and mastering how they can be used.

You can also hook up programs into a pipeline through a pipe, in which the standard output STDOUT of one program feeds directly into the standard input STDIN of another. An example of this could be seen if you were to send your email output to a printer directly. Pipes will be covered in the last section of this lesson.

STDIN

STDIN stands for standard input. The *input connection* for a program is called *STDIN*. A program can expect the incoming data stream from the user (or wherever) to appear at STDIN. User input is read from STDIN. As just mentioned, data can be redirected or piped into a program's STDIN from any source; this was shown with the examples of the `cat` command. The normal input for a program is generally taken from the most common of input peripherals, the keyboard. Remember our last example?

```
> cat  < testfile1  >  testfile2
```

STDIN, when used with `cat` as it is in this example, changes the default input channel to specify a different place to get input from, which happens to be `testfile1` instead of the default, the keyboard.

When you interact with a shell prompt command (like `cat`), the program is reading the data you are entering from STDIN. If you prefer not to enter the data by hand, you can put it in a file and redirect the file into the program's STDIN. The < character directs the contents of the file to its right into the STDIN of the command to the left. Although this is confusing, if you keep reading this over and over and try to apply the concepts to the examples given, I promise you that it will eventually make more sense. Just make sure you are learning the concepts and are able to apply them on this small level. If you can, then move on to more complex command structures, and scripts will almost become commonplace to you. Let's take a look at standard output, STDOUT.

STDOUT

STDOUT stands for standard output. STDOUT is the *output connection* that Unix provides for programs. Just as you can redirect STDIN from a file, if you want to send the output of a command to a file, then you can redirect STDOUT. The > character directs the STDOUT of the program to its left into the contents of the file to its right. In our same example, we look at using the cat command to copy the contents of one file to the contents of another. Commonly, as you saw with cat, used with no argument, its default output was to echo the command back to the terminal. The standard input was the keyboard. Now, the STDOUT has been altered. We learned in the last example that the input (STDIN) was changed to testfile1. Now the standard output (STDOUT) has been changed to testfile2. Getting easier, right?

```
> cat  < testfile1  >  testfile2
```

Again, the standard output is the default output stream that messages are sent to (commonly the end user's terminal). The previous statement, however, redirects the output to testfile2.

 Overwrite or Append?   Using > to redirect output to a text file will overwrite the file if it currently exists (that is, it will replace the file with the new output and the old stuff just goes away). This sort of behavior is not always what one wants, so Unix provides the >> operator as well. Using >> will append, or add on to the end of the existing file any new output redirected to it.

Next up we will learn about the third standard form of I/O, the standard input error, or standard error (STDERR) for short.

STDERR

STDERR is another output stream beyond STDOUT, and it's like that for a good reason. You want the two data streams separated. We already covered STDOUT; it is the first. The second, STDERR, stands for standard input error. STDERR is the output stream that error messages are sent to in Unix. This is commonly the end user's terminal.

If the user is redirecting STDOUT and the program can only put errors on STDOUT, the user might never see the errors that all go into the redirected file. Instead, programs can use STDERR for errors. If the user has not redirected it, then he can still see error messages and warnings while STDOUT is headed into another file or program.

If you want to put STDERR into the same file in which you're storing STDOUT, use >& instead of > in the command; you can do so as follows:

```
> cat < newfile1 >& newfile2
```

Now that we are comfortable with the basics of standard I/O, let's take a look at how to use pipes in Unix.

Pipes

As I keep alluding to, Unix commands alone are powerful, but when you combine them together, you can accomplish complex tasks with ease. The way you combine Unix commands is through using pipes.

To create a pipe in Unix, you simply use a | character between the programs on the command line. A pipe is created by using the keystroke **Shift**+\. This creates a pipe, which looks like this: |. For those of you who are old MS-DOS users, yes, the command has generally the same meaning and is also called a pipe. The pipe, used at the shell prompt, will also help manipulate input. Let's look at an example of a pipe in use:

```
>cat newfile1.txt
Hello
How are you
Fine
>cat newfile1.txt | wc
      1       3       1
```

The word count command (wc) was used with cat and that's what the pipe is good at. Instead of being able to change output from one direction to another based on a file, you can now do the same with commands. This essentially is your primer for joining Unix commands together to unleash even more power under the hood.

We can also pipe into pagers. We learned about pagers earlier in this book. Piping things into pagers is common when you want to view a long listing and do not want it to run off the screen. This was another commonly used MS-DOS command. In Unix, simply type

```
> ls -l | more
```

This looks at your current directory listing, and if it is too long, you can use the more command in conjunction with the ls command to stop the listing at a page. Then you need to press **Enter** or your **spacebar** to cycle through the listing. **Ctrl+z** can break the list if it appears to go on forever.

Watch future examples carefully because the pipe will appear in more useful contexts throughout the rest of the book. In the meantime, make sure that you practice the pipe command with this exercise and master the fundamentals.

Summary

In this lesson, you were introduced to the Unix model of processing input and output, standard I/O, STDIN, STDOUT, STDERR, as well as piping. Here's a review of some of the key points:

- Every program has a STDIN, a STDOUT, and a STDERR. Not all programs use them for user interaction (programs such as Photoshop just don't lend themselves to command-line control), but for the vast majority that do, these input and output connections can be manipulated.

- You can provide the input data that a program expects on STDIN by hand, from a file, or from another program.

- You can send the STDOUT and STDERR of a program into a file if you want to collect it for future use rather than viewing it as it is produced.

- You can pipe the STDOUT of one program into the STDIN of another.

- One immediately useful thing to do with pipes is to pipe the output of particularly verbose programs into a pager (more, less).

LESSON 13
Regular Expressions

In this lesson, you will learn the basics of regular expressions and how to use them in your Unix environment.

As we learn more about Unix, it is apparent that most of its power comes from commands such as cron, ls, man, tail, and so on. And what did we learn in the last lesson? We learned how those commands can be combined or altered based on other characters added, which would specify tasks for Unix. In this chapter, we will continue this discussion, as I will introduce you to the concept of regular expressions.

Regular expressions, commonly known as "RE, RegEx, regexp, regex, or regxp," are a set of key combinations that are meant to allow Unix users and administrators to have control over what they are searching for when using commands such as grep. Regular expressions are used in conjunction with other commands.

Text editors (like vi) and utilities use regular expressions to search and manipulate bodies of text based on certain patterns. Many programming languages, such as Perl, support REs for string manipulation. For example, Perl has a powerful RE engine built directly into its syntax. Although in this lesson you'll be looking primarily at the grep command used in conjunction with REs, you can apply this knowledge to almost everything that uses REs.

Pattern Matching and Regular Expressions

In earlier lessons, you were introduced to the use of the wildcard symbol (*), used to help you find files that you need, or to find contents within a file. Used in conjunction with grep, you can find anything in your Unix system at a very granular level. This, of course, is because of the use of regular expressions. In this section of the lesson, we will look at how to use REs to search for content within a file. This can be helpful if you have saved email you want to parse for information or specific content, or a long file where you are only searching for a company name such as "Que" or "Sams." Using REs, this information can be found quickly. Let's make a file and then use REs to search within it for specific content.

 What Is Perl? Perl is one of the most commonly used web-based programming languages in use today.

Short for Practical Extraction and Report Language, Perl is a programming language developed by Larry Wall. Perl was especially designed for processing text. Because of its strong text-processing capabilities, Perl is one of the most popular languages for writing CGI scripts. Perl is an interpretive language, which makes it easy to build and test simple programs.

Like REs, learning Perl will take some seriously committed time and practice, and a fundamental understanding of programming would be needed for you to understand and learn it. Unfortunately, coverage of both Perl and regular expressions in this chapter is limited as the purpose of the chapter is not for you to master Perl or regular expressions.

Perl comes with many distributions of Unix and Linux. You can learn more about Perl at http://www.perl.org/.

As we just mentioned, REs are a method of specifying a pattern of characters that can then be matched against existing text, so in this example we will make a text file with text that we will specifically search through.

The format for specifying the regular expression in grep is as follows:
grep <regular expression> <filename> <filename> .... Because

this lesson uses grep as its example, familiarize yourself with this format so that you can draw from it as we continue to use it throughout the chapter.

What Is This, Another Root Directory? I am Confused
Do not get overwhelmed by the amount of characters and their meanings all at once. This is what I have found to be one of the biggest hurdles when learning Unix as a beginner—trying to remember the countless commands, their options, dealing with case sensitivity, and now with a whole slew of characters that have meanings and functionality.

In the case with REs, other programs sometimes require that the regular expression be set off with a / on either side of it; this is not the case with grep. Be aware that you may have syntax issues so consult your local man pages and online documentation (or your systems administrator) if you are in a jam.

Using . and *

Let's look at building a new file to practice using regular expressions. In this example, we will use grep in conjunction with the . and * REs. Since REs will specify a method of matching, I will attempt to drive home the concept of REs with a search through a simple text file that you can create with the vi editor or emacs.

Make a file that has the current information within it:

```
Rob's Test File
Rob Shimonski
"aka Unix junkie"
2006
2005
2004
2003
2002
```

```
2001
2000
1999
1899
```

Once you have finished, save and name the file robtest.txt.

This file will serve as the data we will search to learn how to use REs. In this example, we will use the period (.), which can be used to match any character as a single unit, and the asterisk (*), which you can use to match any number of occurrences of a pattern or portion of a pattern. To make this concept easier to understand, let's look at an example of both when using REs with grep to search the robtest.txt file for specific information.

```
> grep "Shimon..." robtest.txt
Rob Shimonski
```

In this example, we saw the use of grep, which was used against the robtest.txt file to search for my last name "Shimonski." It was able to do so, even though I left the last three letters "ski" off, and intentionally put in three periods so that Unix could come back to me with what it found in the robtest.txt file as a match. This can be used in multiple ways, such as the following:

```
> grep "Shimon..i" robtest.txt
Rob Shimonski

> grep "Shi..n.ki" robtest.txt
Rob Shimonski

> grep "S..mo..ki" robtest.txt
Rob Shimonski
```

As you can see, it really doesn't matter what you specify, you just need to specify what is a known exactly as shown in the file so that Unix can find it for you. Unix will attempt to find what it thinks you are looking for, so don't be surprised if you don't narrow your search down and you get thousands of answers from Unix. The period (.) is primarily used to narrow down your search. In cases where you don't really know, and don't mind the possibility of a long and timely search, you can use the asterisk (*).

If you were able to do the first example, then you are definitely able to handle this one because all you are doing is applying a slightly different concept here:

```
> grep "S.*i" robtest.txt
Rob Shimonski
```

With last names like mine, using a wildcard is sometimes your only hope.

Okay, Don't Set Me Off Now!   There are more ways to use grep and REs. This chapter can only cover so much, so it's my intent to interest you and then you can look on your own.

Use \ to set off a special character. Some characters are used by the shell, so they must be escaped by using \. You might want to use this in front of characters that might be special characters as well. In most cases, it doesn't hurt to use \ if you aren't sure. For example, the shell usually expects you to put double quotes (") around strings with spaces in them. It uses the double quotes to group the words in the string. If you need to search through your file for lines containing double quotes, you cannot grep for "; instead, use the following command:

```
> grep \" robtest.txt
"aka Unix junkie"
```

Using the \ in front of the double quotes tells the shell to not attempt to interpret the double quotes normally as a surrounding character, but to instead simply pass it to the grep command for processing.

Using [ ] and ^

In this section, we will learn more about REs, particularly when using and negating ranges using the [ ] and ^ characters.

You've noticed that the robtest.txt file you created and have been using has the years 1899 through 1999 inside of it. We will use grep again in conjunction with REs to match the years that only fall in the 2000 range. To do this, you can specify a range using REs as follows: [*<starting point>*-*<ending point>*]. The starting and ending points can be numbers or ranges within the alphabet.

For example, type the following:

```
> grep "1[8-9]9[0-9]*" robtest.txt
1999
1899
```

This example lets Unix search robtest.txt for anything that is in the 1[8-9][9-0] range, which is only 1999 and 1899. It couldn't be anything from the year 2000 to 2006. The 1 before the bracket specifies that the years can range from either 1[8 which means 18, or 1[9, which specifies 1900. The second bracket specifies the same thing. The second part of the year (the last two digits) has one of them specified already—the 9. Now, apply the same concept. The 9 before the bracket 9[will specify that the last two digits of the year can range anywhere from either 9[0 which means 90, or 9[9, which specifies 1999. Once you have mastered this concept, it should be easier to apply more complex REs.

Using ranges can help you pull certain values out of files that you may need, such as the two years we just showed. You can expand the capability of the range by applying the negation operator as well. The character ^ *negates* a range if it is used at the start of the range specification. Negating a range will match the opposite of what the range matches.

For example, type the following:

```
> grep "1[^8-9]9[0-9]*" robtest.txt
2006
2005
2004
2003
2002
2001
2000
```

Notice that you now match anything that isn't in 1899 through 1999.

Using ^ (Again) and $

Let's learn how to do more with REs, but match the start and end of a line with the ^ (again) and $ characters.

In order to uniquely match the years specified in the sample file, you can use the start-of-line and end-of-line regular expression characters to stop grep from matching items you do not want matched. For example, if my phone number was in the sample file, I would not want it specified and I can do that with REs.

The characters ^ and $ are commonly referred to as *anchors*. To anchor something would be to fix something firmly and stably. They will anchor a pattern to the start or end of a line. 1899 and 1999 are both at the beginning of a line so doing this will not be difficult, and will show you the way these REs are used. These are the two rules you should try to commit to memory when using these characters:

- If ^ is used outside of a range, the ^ character matches the start of a line.

- $ matches the end of a line. If your pattern falls at the end of a line, you can anchor it in this position with $.

For example, examine how this is done:

```
>grep "^1[^7-8][0-9]*" robtest.txt
1899
1999
```

This would have only shown me the dates I specified and nothing else, because I specified it clearly using grep and regular expressions.

Summary

In this lesson, we covered the fundamentals of regular expressions, better known as REs. Regular expressions are an extremely flexible way of describing a pattern to be matched. Because many Unix applications, including the shell, support REs, it is important to develop a general understanding of how they work and what they are used for. With people relying on Unix (or Linux) as their server system or desktop of choice, knowing some of the power you can unleash will aid you in finding areas you need to study deeper, and this is definitely one of them. This lesson was designed to provide enough background for you to begin your true journey into using REs, programming languages like Perl, and beyond into the next lesson's topic: shell scripting with Unix. Here's a review:

- .—This matches any character. Use it whenever you aren't sure what character falls in a specific position.

- *—Using the * matches any number of occurrences of a specific pattern. You can use this in conjunction with . or with ranges.

- \—Special characters need to be escaped using the \ character. If you need to use the quote character (") in a pattern, you'll have to escape it.

- **Ranges**—You can match ranges of numbers or letters to limit a pattern. Ranges are enclosed in [] characters. To negate a range, use ^ at the beginning of the range specification.

- ^/$—These two special characters match the beginning and end of a line, respectively. They are commonly referred to as anchors because they hold a pattern to a specific place on a line.

- **Regular expressions**—These are used in many Unix programs, and can be an extremely powerful tool. Read the man pages for your shell and other utilities in order to determine the extent to which they support regular expressions.

LESSON 14

Shell Scripting Fundamentals

In this lesson, you will learn about the shell and the process of shell scripting to help you automate tasks.

In this chapter, we will cover shell scripting, and really expose some of Unix's true power. We have mentioned shell scripting often in this book, touching upon the subject in almost every lesson and now we finally discuss it. As you may expect, the first lesson in the book could not be on scripting, as you wouldn't know how to log in, what commands you could script with, and all the little odds and ends that are required to build a script. You now have a better understanding, however, as we just had three lessons covering processes, input and output (I/O) control, and regular expressions (REs). Now we tie everything together, and present you with a lesson on the fundamentals of shell scripting.

If you have never worked with a computer before, and this is your first official exposure to scripting, don't panic. It's easily broken down by answering the most common questions.

What is a shell?—A shell is nothing more than a command interpreter. In Unix, the shell is designed to be the interface to the user, to receive the user's input (interpret commands), and act on them. The shell then sends the output to the default, or a specified location, usually the user's terminal. There are some common Unix shells: the C shell, the Bourne shell, and the Korn shell, all of which were covered earlier in the book.

What is a script?—A script is another name for a macro or batch file, which does nothing other than execute what you add to it. If a script is a file, then the contents of the script are essentially what you want to build with Unix commands. That being said, it should make sense that a script is basically a file with a list of commands that can be executed without user interaction. A script language is a simple programming language with which you can write scripts. We covered Perl in the last lesson; this is a commonly used scripting language in Unix environments, and Python is another. You can also develop complex shell scripts right from the shell.

What is a shell script?—Well, if you now know what a shell is, and what a script is, then it should make sense to you that a shell script is nothing more than a script that you create using commands from your current shell (bash, csh, and so on) that the shell in use can interpret. For instance, a shell script written in one shell may not operate properly in a different shell as a different syntax may be used. In any case, you can check your local system's man pages for help if needed.

What is a shell script primarily used for?—Quite simply, (most) scripts are used for automation of tasks. Who wants to type hundreds of lines of text into the shell prompt? No, didn't think you wanted to do that, but what if you put all that into a script (one file) and had that run? Quite possibly with at or cron? The whole picture should be clearing up now.

What is an example of a script in action?—A simple shell script in action is nothing more than picking the shell you are currently working with (I am going to use bash for this example), and knowing what commands you can enter into it. To create a script, you need to know what commands you will enter into it, and what it is going to do beforehand. This way, you don't waste your time writing in your editor or at the shell prompt. If you have a clear picture defined beforehand, then this will save you time and frustration.

Again, a shell script is little more than a list of commands that are run in sequence. Study the man pages to those commands and get all the syntax laid out ahead of time before doing it on the Unix system, especially if it is not a test system and one you use for work or at work.

Conventionally, a shell script should start with a line such as the following:

```
#!/bin/bash
```

This commonly used line will indicate that the script should run in the bash shell regardless of which interactive shell the user has selected. It's important that your commands match the shell or you may see a great many error messages, or quite simply, your script will not work properly. This is very important since the syntax of different shells will almost always vary.

Now, after you set up the script with the correct indicator of what shell to use, enter some commands.

```
#!/bin/bash
echo "Hi this is Unix speaking, I know who you are, you are
$USER"
echo "Your current directory is also known, it happens to be,
$PWD"
ls  # note script used to check user, directory and list files
```

Whoa, what do we have here? Well, without panicking (this is common to do when you see something like this) pick it apart, piece by piece.

The first line sets the shell. The second line uses the $USER variable to echo back your current username (in this case I happen to be logged in as root). The third line is identical to the second except you see the $PWD variable in use; this tells you your current directory location. The fourth line tells Unix to list the contents of the current directory. Doing each of these commands one at a time will simulate the script executing one line at a time. This can also all be placed in one file (master emacs or vi) and executed as a script file by a user or another program like at or cron.

Remember, this script should be populated with commands that bash can handle and process; therefore, this is why you may not have noticed some of these commands or they may not be available on your version of Unix. This is why it is important to master the basics so you can do scripting in the first place. As you can see from our example, some comfort with your shell is needed.

Keep going over this example until you understand it completely. It is important to learn how to do scripts if you are going to be a Unix administrator. For end users, you may never need to create a script, but you may consider that your current employer expects you to come in every day and run a certain amount of jobs. Remember the jobs command? That could be added to a script and automated with at or cron. This is your call, but scripting is something I would learn in more depth. Scripting is a powerful aspect of Unix, and is one of the things that separates the men and women from the mice.

What Is All This Gibberish?   No, don't bash your head into a wall to try to understand this; it happens to be specific to bash and not Unix in general. That's why we talked about shells in the beginning of the book; it is important that you know that they are different. When a shell is chosen, or given to you by default, using scripts from one shell to another can be problematic. In the bash shell script example just covered, the last line in the script had a number sign (#) after the ls command. If you ran the script (and the syntax was entered correctly), the # reflects what is known as a comment. If you are an experienced Microsoft Windows user, you may have had to edit a file and you saw the # used to make a comment.

Comments are common when programming or scripting because you sometimes need to leave yourself a note as to what a line of the script of the code does. In this case, I made it very simple. The ls command is used to list files, and the comment specified that. The comment will be seen by Unix, but not repeated on the screen like the echo command performed.

Other items that may be foreign to you are the $USER and $PWD elements. These are environment variables, which respectively represent what user is currently logged in and executing the script and tell you what directory you may be in, such as /etc or /, for example. These variables produce output similar to the whoami and pwd commands.

If you have absorbed everything up to now, you will be writing scripts in no time at all. There is just not enough space here to cover all the little nuances between shells, and to cover everything you can do with scripting would take a lifetime. In any case, you should now feel comfortable with what a shell script is, understand all the terminology revolving around it, and how to define one in your shell of choice.

 Have You Seen This Before?   You may be wondering where you have seen this before. Scripting is common in MS-DOS.

If you are familiar with MS-DOS, then you will notice that shell scripts are similar to batch files. If you are familiar with *.bat files, then you know what I mean.

Building Unix Shell Script Files

In our shell script example, we saw that lines of text (such as commands with REs) could be entered into the shell prompt (command interpreter) and executed. This is not necessarily a script file because it is not in a file. It's just being added to the prompt and executed immediately.

The other way to do this would be to use those lines (so you don't have to type them) to identically add them to a file that you can run to execute its contents. In other words, when you boot up your system and login, you can have your email opened, and run a cron job, maybe open the vi editor—you add all these to the file, save it, and then run that file. By typing the name of the file at the shell prompt, it will execute the file's contents, which should be multiple commands and REs. You have just entered the ranks of the prestigious, the *shell scripter*.

Once constructed and saved, your script will produce exactly the results outlined at the beginning of this section. Again, make sure that you run the correct script against the correct shell.

Using `foreach`

When you find yourself putting in commands over and over, you can use the `foreach` statement that executes a code block for each data item in an array. An array is a set of elements indexed sequentially that have the same type of data. Most times, each element of an array has a unique identifying index number. Changes made to one element of an array do not affect the other elements. `foreach` specifies that for each entry in the array of entries, Unix will output the entries to the terminal. Commonly, `foreach` is used in place of a standard `for` loop. Unlike this `for` loop construct, however, a `foreach` loop usually does not specify the order in which the items are considered.

The point of this is, if you don't want to spend a massive amount of time inputting files into a command to automate them, you can use the `foreach` command, which takes a list of files, and does something "for each" of them based on what you specify. The commands' use is much easier to demonstrate than to explain. If you have a list of files that you need to do something to, you can follow these steps to use `foreach`:

1. Figure out what you want to do. In the following example, you've got a bunch of directories (1 through 3), and you want to create a `tar` file of each of them.

2. Decide on the names of the files/directories that you want to do something to. In this case, you're going to create `tar` files for the directories `directory1`, `directory2`, and `directory3`.

3. Pick a variable name that you want to use. For this example, you're going to use a variable named `test`. It doesn't matter what the variable name is, as long as it doesn't conflict with the name of the command.

4. Issue the `foreach` command as `foreach <variablename>` `(<filenames>)`. The `foreach` command then asks what you want to do for each file by displaying a question mark. Fill this in with whatever you need to do. Again, you're going to be `tar`ing files in the example. After giving `foreach` the command for whatever it is you want to do, finish it by putting the command `end` on a line by itself.

This can be seen as

```
> foreach test (directory1 directory2 directory3)
? tar -cvf $test.tar $test
? end
```

Your machine responds by running the `tar` command for each file you gave it to work with. Inside the `foreach` command loop, note the use of the expression *$test*. `foreach` goes through the list of filenames you gave it and puts each one sequentially in the test variable. To use the contents of a variable in the shell, put a $ sign before it. For example, `foreach` first puts `mydirectory1` in the variable test. It then runs the `tar` command, and the shell expands the test variable to `directory1`. The `tar` command that gets executed actually looks like the following: `tar -cvf mydirectory.tar mydirectory`. The next time through the loop, `foreach` puts `directory2` in the variable test, and the process is repeated.

You can use REs in the shell instead of enumerating the filenames to use the `foreach` command. If you notice in the previous example, all the directories you want to `tar` actually have part of their names in common *directory*. If you wanted to produce the same results without having to enumerate all the directory names to `foreach`, you might issue the preceding `foreach` command as follows: `foreach test (*directory)`.

What Shell Should I Use? In some examples, you may see the C shell used (csh). It is the opinion of this author that csh is a tool not adequate for programming and learning shell scripting. Also, it is better for you to learn on the shell you know, or a commonly used and supported shell, especially if you are a new learner to Unix. The use of csh to create shell scripts should be avoided if you can. The use of csh to build simple scripts is cumbersome, problematic, and sometimes next to impossible.

It's easy to see how you can use Unix to control process, and now, you should start to see the granular level of control Unix can give you over what it is you do work on. You can fine-tune, tweak, and customize your system once you know how to master these fundamentals. Now that you are familiar with the `foreach` command, let's look at conditional statements such as `while` and `if`.

Using `while` and `if`

If you want to build more complex scripts, you can use other statements to control your automations. You can turn to conditional statements that allow you to activate certain sections of your script only when certain conditions apply. To use conditional statements, you need to create a condition for the statement to test. This lesson covers the basics; just be aware that this can get in-depth as there are many operators, and different items of syntax you can work with.

 Hello Operator?   Almost all programming languages in existence have a set of operators that perform arithmetical operations. Computers are mathematical devices, which function based on Boolean math.

The `if` command works in much the same way as the `while` command, except it doesn't loop; it simply executes one command based on the condition. The syntax of the `if` command is as follows: `if ( <condition> ) <command>`. The `while` command, with the syntax `while (<condition>)`, does things while a certain condition holds.

To set up a conditional statement, you can check out the following syntax, which is based on `if` and evaluates an expression placed in parentheses as seen here:

```
if ( the expression )
actionA
[else
actionB]
```

If the expression evaluates as true, then the first action (`actionA`) is done. The other clause you can specify is `else`, which makes sense when you say it verbally outside of typing it in the Unix shell prompt.

"If you don't have the key, `then` you don't get in." Easy enough, right?

- `actionA`: lost key

- `actionB`: no enter

That should wrap up the `if` statement for you. Again, this can get more complex, but for this lesson, you should feel comfortable with using the `if` statement when building a shell script.

Summary

In this lesson, we covered what you need to know to get started, and how Unix works with writing complex scripts. We also looked at a sample script and dissected it so that its contents made sense. Shell scripting is an advanced topic and was covered only briefly here, so please take the time if it interests you and expand your learning on it. There are many online tutorials and books available to help you learn your favorite shells' scripting capabilities. Here's a review of the key points of this lesson:

- Your shell scripts can be stored in files to enable you to execute many commands by simply typing one. You already know how to make a file; now you are starting to learn what to populate it with.

- There are many different shells and your shell might work differently than what is presented here, but probably has similar capabilities. You need to select and use a shell that serves your needs, and then learn the scripting functionality of that shell.

- The `foreach` command enables you to repeat a set of commands for each of a number of files.

- The `while` command enables you to repeat a set of commands while a certain condition holds.

- The `if` command enables you to execute a command, or not execute it, based on a conditional statement.

LESSON 15
User Utilities

In this lesson, you will learn how to change settings on your Unix system and modify or alter your environment.

When working with Unix, you will undoubtedly come to a point where some form of customization is required. For instance, we talked about logging in to your Unix system, but what about changing your password? We have also discussed the shell many times, especially in the last lesson on shell scripting, but what if you want to change your shell? These and other methods of customization will be discussed within this chapter.

Using chsh

In our discussion of shells earlier in this book, we have talked many times about either what shell you are using or what shell prompt commands you can perform. We have also touched on why you may want to change your shell, and now we will cover how to do just that within your Unix environment.

In the beginning of this book, you learned that there are a variety of different shells that you can run; we covered most if not all of them. There will be times when you will want to change your shell, and to do that, you can use the change shell command, or chsh. The chsh command will allow you to choose one of the shells that is registered for use on your machine. This means that you must have a shell on your system in order to request it.

One problem you may encounter is not knowing which shell to choose; after all, there are so many shells, and how do you know which ones are registered for use on your system? To help solve this problem, you can use the chsh command with the -1 option. The chsh -1 command will list out all the available shells on your system. After using chsh -l, changing shells is as easy as running the correct command and knowing what syntax to use.

```
>chsh -l

/bin/ash
/bin/bash
/bin/csh
/bin/ksh
/bin/sh
/bin/bsh
/bin/tcsh
/bin/zsh
```

In this example, there are eight different shells that you can choose from. If you wanted to change to the bash shell from your current shell, you would do the following:

```
>chsh

Changing shell for rob.
Password: *****
New shell [/bin/csh]: /bin/bash
Shell changed.
```

The next time you logged in to your machine, you would be in the bash shell instead of your previous shell. You probably won't ever need to change your shell unless the default shell on your system is not able to do what you want it to.

The Shell Game   Changing your shell is easy, but it all depends on your distribution of Unix or Linux and how it is set up. In some distributions, you may find yourself locked out of your session if you make a mistake. Again, this illustrates the need to practice on a Unix system that you are not working on just in case you do make a mistake and wind up in a jam. There is absolutely no shame in asking for help if you don't know what you are doing. Practice makes perfect, so I suggest getting yourself a lab system and changing into all the shells just to see how to do it.

Now that you have changed the default shell in your Unix system, you can either keep it that way or change it back. For the next portion of the lesson, you should be in the shell most comfortable to you. If you changed into a shell you are not familiar with, you should change back to the shell that you usually work in so that you can follow the rest of the lesson's exercises.

The passwd Command

As covered in the first lesson, it's imperative that you have a set of credentials in order to log in to a Unix system. Credentials consist of a username (usually assigned to you by your Unix system administrator) and a password. Although the password is generally configured by the system administrator, you can change it yourself. More specifically, if your machine is not connected to a network with other Unix computers, then you can use the passwd command to change your password.

There Are Other Ways to Change   If you are not on a standalone Unix system and are connected to other systems through a network (which is a way to use wired or wireless connections to allow systems to share resources), there is a way to change your password in what is called the Network Information Service (NIS) database. The yppasswd utility changes network passwords associated with the usernames in the NIS database. Although this concept is pretty far beyond the level of knowledge covered in this book, it's important to mention in case you come across it instead of the passwd command. There are also other syntaxes for the yppasswd command, such as uypasswd for example. Because passwords may be stored on multiple machines, this utility will update your password on all systems on which you may be working. Check your local man pages for more information on using these commands.

To use the `passwd` command, you must first have the proper privileges to make a change. If you are not a SuperUser (su), `passwd` will first prompt you for your current password just to make sure you are who you say you are (this is a security measure implemented to protect your credentials), and Unix *will not* continue unless the correct password is entered.

After you enter your current password, you will be asked for your new password, as shown in the following example:

```
>passwd

Changing password for rob
Old password: *****
New password: ******
Retype new password: ******
Password successfully changed
```

Choose a Good Password   Choosing a new password should be something that you take seriously so that you can protect access to your Unix system.

Your new password should be at least six characters long and not purely alphabetic. You should use numbers as well as upper- and lowercase letters (Unix is case sensitive!) or special signs such as # or @ in your password. Doing so will help keep your password safe.

Try to avoid the obvious when choosing your password. For instance, if you have pictures of your cat Fluffy all over your office or cubicle, then a password of "fluffy" is not going to keep your Unix system safe. The name of your favorite baseball team or your children's names are also bad choices for passwords unless you enjoy being a victim. Also, don't just append a 1, then a 2, and so on to your password when you are forced to change it (for example, fluffy1, fluffy2, fluffy3, and so on). Make sure you always use strong passwords and don't let anyone steal them from you; that way, you can ensure that nobody uses your passwords for improper purposes.

The passwords you type are not shown on your display as you type them; this way, if someone is looking over your shoulder, they cannot see what you type, and Unix offers no clues to your would-be attacker. In this example, asterisks (*) are used to indicate that typing has taken place. If the password change is successful, Unix indicates that with a message such as, "Password successfully changed." If not, you will see another message, most likely "Authentication Failure" if you did not supply the correct credentials needed to successfully change your password.

In some cases, Unix can keep you from choosing certain passwords if they are too short or based on words in Unix's built-in dictionary file. If your Unix machine is set up this way and you enter an unacceptable password, the `passwd` command usually tells you what you need to do to correct it. Choose passwords that mix letters, numbers, and letter cases and that are not based on common words.

Using `finger` and `chfn`

In the Unix environment, you are able to use a tool called `finger` to list user information. Although this is a dangerous command to leave unsecured, it's helpful to some degree. Most times, `finger` is disabled because if left open and unmanaged, it can be exploited. For this reason, we will not spend too much time on `finger`; you most likely may not even be able to use it on your system. If you can, you will see that in cases in which no other way to list information is available (like an email or messaging application), `finger` does the job quite nicely.

How does `finger` work? To put it in simple terms, information about each user's physical address is stored as part of the user's system password file when populating the `finger` database; this means that it is possible to retrieve information about each user from the `finger` database—it's that easy. If you are performing `finger` on your own system (by typing **finger** and pressing **Enter**), you should see a summary detailing your login, name, login time, and where you are logged in from.

If you use `finger` on your own system and do not get the information you desire, you only need to populate the appropriate fields, thus completing the information. Remember, though, this information can be publicly accessed. In order to change the information, you'll need to use `chfn`, which is discussed later in the lesson.

Using the `finger` command is simple. Just enter **finger <username>** to get information about a user who is local to your system. To get information about someone on a remote system, try entering the following: **finger <username>@<remote host>**. Depending on the type of remote host and how the remote host is configured, this command might or might not work.

Let's look at the following example:

```
rshimonski@UNIX1>finger

Login: Name:          Idle: Login Time: Where:
rob ___Rob Shimonski___-___Fri 18:23  Console
```

This is the `finger` information returned about my personal account. As you can see, there isn't much here other than my login name, my user account name (full name here), my status, the time I logged in, and the location from where I logged in. This is all that is returned because I have not yet set any other personal information. In the next section, we will learn to use the `chfn` command to add more information to an account. You will only be able to add this information if you are working in a lab environment or have permission to do so (that is, if your system even continues to use `finger` in the first place).

 Finger Is Normally Disabled As previously mentioned, `finger` is usually disabled on most Unix systems. Most system administrators who audit their Unix systems for security holes consider this particular protocol to be exploitable, so many times, they disable this function.

Using `chfn`

The `chfn` command runs an interactive process that enables you to set more personal information into your account. That way, when you run `finger`, you can get more detail. Run `chfn` on a command line without any options, as follows:

```
>chfn

Changing finger information for rob.
Password: *****
Enter the new value, or press ENTER for the default
Full Name: Robert Shimonski
Room Number: 13
Work Phone: (212)123-4567
Home Phone: (212)234-5678
Other: 0
Finger information changed.
```

Once you see "Finger information changed," you can run `finger` again and view the changes that you made. Again, although this command is helpful, it's not often used in light of today's messaging applications and portable databases that can be accessed using mobile phones, pocket PCs, and so on.

> **Disable `finger`**   Many Unix and Linux distributions install default services that are little used and have a poor security history. As security becomes more of an issue, you may find yourself sitting at one of the most locked-down systems you have ever seen. Why? For one, the protocol based around the `finger` utility is as insecure as someone standing over your shoulder trying to capture your credentials as you type them.
>
> In addition, `finger` uses clear text (not encrypted text) by default and has notoriously been the target of hackers. Because `finger` is a program that displays information about a particular user or all users logged on to a system, it would make sense that it would be the target of any hacker, attacker, or exploiter of good. Unless disabled, `finger` will continue to be a source of good information for these individuals.

So now that you know how to change your shell and alter your password and personal information, let's turn our attention to monitoring your Unix system. In the next section, we will cover a few commands that can help you manage Unix. They are `date`, `uptime`, and `who`.

Using date

The `date` command will either return the current date and time or allow you to change them. You can only change the date if you have proper permission to do so. It is important to have the correct date on your system because so many specific things rely on time to function properly. For instance, consider event logs. If you want a record of events such as security issues in your Unix system, you would want those entries to show up in the log, of course. You would want to know, for example, that someone was trying to enter your Unix system without permission. However, even if you have your system set up to log such events, the log entries will be of little use if the time and date on your system are not correct. For instance, if the time and date are incorrect, you may not notice someone trying to log in to your system with your username and password in the middle of the night (a clear indicator of someone trying to hack in during off-hours). Even if you do notice this attempt, you will not know the exact time that it took place. Without solid logs that are provable, you do not have much of a leg to stand on.

If you have the right privileges, you can use `date` to see and set the day and time on your Unix system. Ordinary user accounts do not have this capability and won't be able to use this command. If you have proper privileges, you can view or change your date by typing the following:

```
>date
Sat April 01 06:30:01 EDT 2005
```

There's nothing to it. Remember, the `date` command is used to check and set your date. If you are running a GUI (such as KDE or GNOME), just check the right corner of your panel taskbar. You should see the time and date; if not, then just open a shell prompt and type the `date` command.

Using `uptime`

`uptime` is another simple and useful command that can be used to verify how long your Unix system has been up and running. The `uptime` command returns the current time, the number of users logged in to the system, how long the system has been running, and the amount of load that the system is under. Just type **uptime** at the command prompt, as follows:

```
>uptime
6:30am up 12:50, 3 users, load average: 0.15, 0.11, 0.04
```

In this example, we can see that `uptime` returns the current time, up since, how many users are currently logged in to Unix, and the load average. Just about everything here should be self-explanatory except for the load average. The load average is composed of three values: the first value is the load on the system during the past minute, the second value is the load average during the last 10 minutes, and the third value is the load average during the last 15 minutes. These values are rarely more than one or two. If you see a system load average of anything more than five, your computer is busy, and you may see performance degradation.

Using `who`

In addition to `date` and `uptime`, there is another Unix command that can help you manage your system. This command is called `who`. This is not the same as `whoami`, a command you learned earlier in this book. The `whoami` command returns only the username of the person currently logged in and accessing the shell prompt. By using `who`, you can see more information.

Unix is a multiuser system; this means that there can be many different users logged in at any given time. Therefore, it's important to know how to see who is also logged in to your system, and you can do this by using the `who` command. Use this command as follows:

```
>who

rob      pts/0 April 7, 2005 (console)
mary     pts/1 April 7, 2005
jane     pts/2 April 7, 2005
admin    pts/3 April 7, 2005
```

This example shows that there are currently four users logged in to the system. who returns the username of each user who is logged in, as well as the name of the controlling terminal, the date and time that the users logged in, and sometimes the IP address from which the users are connected. Each version of Unix or Linux may produce different output, so visit your local man pages for more information on the who command.

Summary

In this lesson, we covered the use of Unix system utilities such as chsh, passwd, finger, date, who, and uptime. There are more utilities to choose from and use, but for a 10-minute lesson, this is plenty of information to digest and practice with. Remember, practice makes perfect, so make sure that you spend time using these commands; they are all helpful and will serve you well when needed, especially passwd. In fact, you should spend the greatest amount of time with the passwd command and master its usage, syntax, and available options.

The following is a quick review of what was covered in this lesson:

- **chsh**—Use the chsh command to change your current shell. If you don't know which shell you want to switch to, you can use chsh -l to list the available shells on your system.

- **passwd/yppasswd**—The passwd command changes your account password. If you're in an environment with networked Unix computers, you might have to use the yppasswd command instead.

- **finger**—This command looks up personal information about an account on your computer or on a remote computer. finger is sometimes disabled for security reasons, so you might not be able to use this command to get the results you expect.

- **chfn**—You can change finger information using this command. For example, you can change your full name, your office address, and your office and home phone numbers in your account profile by using chfn.

- **date**—Simply enough, date displays the current day and time on your computer.

- **uptime**—The uptime command provides a summary of information about the state of your operating system, including the length of time it has been online, the number of users currently logged in, and the average load on your system during the past 15 minutes.

- **who**—who enables you to see all the users who are logged in to your computer, the date that they connected, and the network address from which they are connected. If your machine seems slow, you might want to use who to find out where all the processor time is going.

LESSON 16
Modifying Your Environment

In this lesson, you'll learn more about how to work with the Unix user environment.

Unix is flexible if you know how to bend it. In this lesson, we will continue to bend it with helpful commands that will allow you to modify your user environment. We will cover commands from alias commands that help you shorten what you type, all the way to setting environment variables and paths. Finally, we will cover user defaults in the form of dot files, as well as how to alter things within the GUI and the KDE.

Aliases

To use aliases, you must first understand what an alias is. An alias is a file that represents another object in the file system. For example, if you specify a file that just says grepnow, inside it you may have a complex grep command with REs (regular expressions) and/or many options. Typing **grepnow** at the shell prompt will execute that file's contents, which will be the longer command. What would you rather type out?

```
grepnow
grep "[:digit:]\{3\}[ -]\?[:digit:]\{4\}" file
```

The choice is clear. Using aliases can really save you time on frequently entered commands, especially if they are long in syntax.

Suppose you want to match a specific number of repetitions of a pattern. A good example is a phone number. You could easily search for a 7-digit phone number using this methodology. One of the most useful features that shells provide to the user is the capability to create command aliases. As you can see, the commands can get completely out of hand as you use REs and options to build it out and make it more effective.

Aliases are, quite simply, aliases. If, for example, you're a longtime DOS user, you might find yourself typing **del** instead of **rm** to delete files. Want to change this? Just set an alias with the alias command. The syntax is as follows: alias `<newname> <command to run>`. If you actually want to make that alias for del, type the following: **alias del rm**. After setting this alias, any time you type **del**, it executes the command rm. This is actually something commonly done on many different systems.

More useful than simply renaming commands, you can use the alias command to create *meta* commands that enforce certain options. For example, it's always a good idea to force rm to be in interactive mode (rm -i). To do this with an alias, you can type the following: **alias rm 'rm -i'**. (Note the direction of the single quotes.) Now when you type rm it actually executes rm -i instead.

Remember, aliasing is done to help you shorten your typing workload. If you find yourself in situations where you are typing out long strings often and they all start to look identical, then it would make sense to create aliases to save you some time.

Environment Variables

Earlier in this book, we touched on the concept of environmental variables in Unix. In Lesson 14, "Shell Scripting Fundamentals," variables used in the shell were discussed. To explain how environment variables are used, consider how your Unix system runs. Most of the programs are configured to run based on text files that help build the command into the environment for use. If you don't have a file, then most likely you will be setting a program up with an environmental variable. The environmental variable will essentially be where the program draws its essential configuration information from.

Environment variables are used by programs to pick up specific pieces of information that are needed when the program is run. For example, you might run across some programs that want an environment variable that contains the path to their help-file information and if not, they will not work when asked for help. This is a common issue revolving around the path usage. Remember, it is important to understand what the path is. This is another special shell variable called the *path variable*. It tells the shell where to look for programs that you want to execute. In this next example, we will look at the syntax of setting your environmental variables.

Environment variables aren't set using quite the same syntax as regular shell variables, so instead of using set `<variablename>=<value>`, use the following syntax:

`setenv <variablename> <value>`.

 What Is an Environment Variable? Environmental variables are used by your Unix system to pass information to programs and customize their behavior.

When working with environmental variables, you should really work in a lab environment and test changes to the environment until you get used to making these changes. Absolute beginners on Unix should show caution when altering user environment settings and should always write down the changes they make; it is easy to be overwhelmed quickly.

The possibilities are endless, making settings changes easy.

 What's Good for the Goose May Not Be Good for You When working with environmental variables, you need to consider the following. Remember that the settings you make in one shell do not affect other shells. If you need to access more than one configuration at a time, you can have the same environment variable set to different values in different shells you're running simultaneously.

Paths

As was just mentioned, a path tells the shell where to look for programs that you want to execute. You might notice that if you have a copy of a program in your current directory, typing the filename sometimes results in a `command not found` error. This is because it's common for the path variable to lack the current directory. A good way to simulate this problem is to type the following:

```
> \(-
> (-: Command not found
```

In addition to getting a nice smiley face you can see that there is no command found for this entry. All this means is that you either don't have a path or you don't have a command. You can execute programs in the current directory by typing `./<program>` or by adding the current directory to your path. The current directory is usually left out of the path because including it could be a security risk. Because working with Unix implies knowing a little about security and how to protect Unix, you should be aware of why you may not have a command present if needed, or an option available that you may need or want.

If your current directory is in your path, you can potentially be fooled into executing arbitrary programs by naming them as common Unix commands, and sneaking them into your directories as aliases or script files, which is not good.

If you want to see what your current path is, you can do so by using `echo $PATH`. If it's missing some paths you need, the current directory and `/usr/local/bin`, for example, you can add these by using the following command:

```
set path=($path /usr/local/bin .)
```

Now that you are familiar with working with a path and viewing it, let's take a look at your Unix user defaults and dot files.

Using Dot Files

When a new Unix system user account is created, certain default settings maintained in default configuration files (called dot files) are placed in the user's home directory (~). Dot files are files with names starting with the . character. Depending on the Unix shell in use, different files are more active than others. For the most part, these files should be left alone unless you know what you are doing. However, there will be times when you will need to alter them although frequent changes to these files are not needed.

In working with dot files, you may accidentally corrupt them or make them invalid with an incorrect entry. Invalid or corrupted dot files can prevent you from logging in or otherwise affect your account. It is important that you back these up, and that you tread carefully when making changes at work. However, if you have the time and patience, have a free-for-all on your Unix home lab system. To list all of your dot files, type **ls -a** at the shell prompt.

Use Combined Options   When you want to see your dot files in a long listing, type **ls -la**. The . is what makes them hidden files.

Not all systems have examples you can follow, but for those of you who do: What are some of the default dot files you think you may encounter? Following is a list of some of the default dot files you are likely to see, use, or come in contact with sometime on your Unix system.

- **.login** and **.logout**—As you might guess, .login and .logout files are executed when you log in and when you log out. If you look in these files, you will find that they are shell scripts, which use commands that you are familiar with.

- **.cshrc** or **.profile**—Shell scripts that are executed when you open a shell. Shells have their own scripts that execute at startup.

- **.X11defaults** or **.Xdefaults**—This file contains settings that are used by the server resource database; the settings are mainly used in the X Window System.

If you use the find command with a wildcard such as find *.* /etc, you can see that many dot files are in your directories as well. Don't be afraid to look in the dot files; just don't alter them if you do not know what you are doing, or if you are on a production system at work that you cannot test on.

Working with the GUI

Like most desktop environments, KDE includes the capability to customize your desktop environment just as you do under Windows or any other desktop operating system. Some form of alteration is allowed depending on your permissions. You can set items such as the background wallpaper for your viewing pleasure, screensavers, fonts, and many other things. Because there is so much to work out in KDE, let's take a look at a simple exercise that allows you to change some of KDE's default configurations for your shell. This is shown in Figure 16.1.

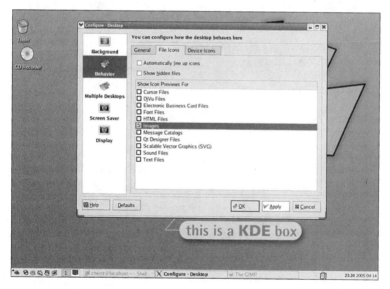

FIGURE 16.1 Use KDE to make changes to the default configuration.

Use the following steps to change KDE's default preview behavior:

1. Right-click on the **KDE desktop**.

2. Click on **Behavior** on the left.

3. Select the types of files you would like KDE to create previews for.

4. Make the changes you want, and then click the **Apply** or **OK** button to set them.

Summary

In this lesson, we looked at how to modify your user environment and what is needed to customize it. Although we skimmed only the surface, you should feel comfortable enough to make some configuration changes on your system. You are also advised to practice these on a system where harmful changes won't cause too much of a problem. Use a lab whenever you can.

The following was covered in this lesson:

- Environment variables are always uppercase, and preceded by $. This is how they are identified as variables.

- Environment variables are frequently used for specifying single configuration options to a program, such as providing a pointer to a directory that the program needs.

- The $PATH variable keeps track of where the system searches for commands when you type them. If a command exists on the system, but the path to the command is not in your $PATH variable, it will not be found when you type the command name.

- Aliases are a very powerful feature of Unix shells. They enable you to rename commands, or cause commands to always use certain options when you issue them.

- Dot files are everywhere. Many programs use text files containing configuration information for control purposes. These files almost universally have filenames, which start with a . character. They are the place to look for automating settings to your shell, and for configuring options for the windowing system.

LESSON 17
Printing with Unix

In this lesson, you'll learn how to print with your Unix system.

This lesson doesn't cover system administration–level work such as installing and deploying printers but how you, the Unix user, interface with a printer already configured for operation.

Similar to how Unix views everything as a file, Unix also views printing differently and does not create a difference between printing locally and remotely. Because of this, a printer can be physically attached to your system, or not attached to your system but attached to another system, or merely a device put on the network itself.

Quick History Lesson   In the past, there have been two different Unix printing methodologies: the lp system and the lpd system. lpd was created on the Berkeley Standard Distribution (BSD) Unix and lp was created on the AT&T System V.

Since the lp system is older and less functional, this chapter will primarily focus on the use of lpd. If you are still trapped into using lp, this chapter can help you, but it's better if you consult your man pages as well.

Now, let's look at how to send a print job using the lpr command.

The `lpr` Command

Because Unix is a multiuser environment, it would only make sense that more than one person would be printing to a printer at any single time. When you print in Unix, your print job is sent with a print job number. This number is assigned to the job by Unix to track and complete the job. Canceling a print job after you start one is canceled based on that job number. The job is removed from the print queue and then you no longer have a print job pending.

Now that you understand the fundamentals of printing in Unix, let's take a look at how to actually get it done.

With the `lpd` (line printer daemon and its protocol) system available on your machine, you can use the `lpr` suite of commands to send print jobs to your printer. The `lpr` (*line printer*) command is the primary method for sending data to the printer and is available on most, if not all, Unix systems unless disabled or removed. `lpr` essentially dumps all data directly to the printer that you specify. To use `lpr`, follow these steps:

1. Determine the name of the printer you want to use. In some cases, your Unix system administrator will give you the name.

2. Choose the file you want to print such as a text file. If you do not have one to print, make one with `emacs` or `vi`.

3. Send the print job by using the following command: `lpr -P<printer name> <filename> <filename>`.... (There is no space between the `-P` and the printer name.)

4. If there is only one printer configured on your computer, chances are you can simply type **`lpr <filename> <filename>`**....

Let's look at an example of how to print out a print job. As an example, type the following:

```
>lpr -Ppr1 anyfile.txt
```

Printing, Printer, Print Server, Print Queue... What?
There are a lot of terms to understand, and if you
really want to learn how printing works you will need
to know the details. Printing can be confusing if you
do not understand all the terminology revolved
around it.

For one, *printing* is the process for reproducing copies
of texts and images on the Unix system. A *printer* is
the device used to do the actual printing work. A
printer is a peripheral hardware device that produces
a hard copy (permanent human-readable text and/or
graphics, usually on paper) from data stored in a computer connected to it or from another source. A *print
server* is generally the computer and/or software that
is used to provide users or a network with access to a
central printer. The print server shares resources and
collects its jobs in its *print queue* (mostly found on the
print server but in some cases can also be on the local
system). The print server then sends the print jobs to
the hardware printer. The printer server acts as a
buffer, holding the information to be printed out in
memory until the printer is free and clear. It is possible
to program the print server to print jobs in the order
they arrive, or to give priority to particular users who
need it. If you need to remove a job from the queue,
only the root user or the person who owns a print job
can remove it from the queue. A *print job* is the job
you sent to the printer. The job is nothing more than
what you want done.

This should clear things up so you can master the rest
of the lesson. Make sure you clearly understand these
definitions before moving on.

The result of this command is that the file anyfile.txt is sent to the
printer named pr1. If the printer is not busy, then the print job will be
printed immediately. If the need arises, you may need to print multiple
copies of a document. You can do this by entering the same command
once for each copy you need, or by simply specifying the number of
copies as an option to the lpr command.

No Print Job for You! You may not be able to print because you are not configured to do so. Running the lpr command may give you an error such as "no default destination available" or some other error (it will be different based on your Unix version) that simply states that you do not have a destination device for your hardware printer to send the job to. Because of this, Unix just tells you "sorry—no print job for you!"

Specify the number of copies as an option to the lpr command by doing the following: type **lpr** with **-#<number of copies>** to print that many copies of each file in the job. That's it!

Also, there are a few file formats and special print cases that might require special attention from the print command. *Filters* are applied to a file to convert the information to a special format. The format can be any that the printer can handle. Here are a few examples of common filters:

- **.ps**—This extension stands for postscript files. Postscript files will be handled automatically by the lpr command. You can print them as you print a plain text file.

- **.dvi**—This extension stands for text files. Files from text contain special page layout instructions. You can use the -d option with lpr in order to print these files correctly.

- **.tr**—This extension stands for troff files. This is the standard file format for man pages. You can use the -t option to print out a man page.

Now you know how to print with Unix, and some of the commands you can use to send jobs to a printer. We now need to know how to check the status of a print job, so that if a problem occurs it can be dealt with quickly.

My Cups Runneth Over...   CUPS, or the Common Unix Printing System, also uses filters. CUPS is the newer model that Unix and Linux are based on, which is more standardized.

CUPS is a modular Unix printing system that allows your system to act as a print server. CUPS was designed to be easier to network than standard Unix printing solutions. CUPS consists of a Unix print spooler, a scheduler, as well as a filtering system.

When using CUPS, you will see a big advantage in that it can process a variety of formatted data to the print server through the use of its filters. It converts the print job data into the format the printer will under-stand. CUPS does this using MIME (Multipart Internet Mail Extensions) types. MIME is an Internet Standard for the format of email, but is commonly used in other systems to determine the type of file that is being processed.

Spooling   A print spooler is a program that holds (stores) documents that are to be printed. This is the program that manages the handling of the data from the print requestor (you), to the print device (the printer). Jobs are spooled into the queue where they await their turn to print.

The `lpq` Command

You send the job to the printer, what next? Well, the print job can be checked to see if it's in fact in the queue and being processed by the print server. After you've sent a job to the printer, especially if it is a network printer located a distance away, you will want to verify the completion of a job so that you know if you need to send it again or check for other problems.

To check the status of a job, you'll want to look at the queue for the printer to which you submitted the job. You do this with the `lpq -P<printer name>` command. Once again, if there is only a single printer on your system, you can probably just issue `lpq` by itself.

Type the following:

```
>lpq -Ppr1

Rank    Owner      Job  Files                      Total Size
1st     rob         27    testfile.txt              100 bytes
2nd     erika       28    anyfile.txt             30023 bytes
```

This example shows that there are currently two different jobs in the printer queue for pr1. One is owned by myself (rob), and the user erika owns the second. Each job is ranked; this shows the order in which it will print. The names of the files being printed are also shown, as are the size and job ID number.

So now you know how to start a print job and check the status of it, but what if you wanted to stop or cancel your print job? What do you do?

The `lprm` Command

If you send a job to a printer and it isn't what you wanted, you can cancel it. This is common in times when you are rushing and you press **Print** and realize, "I didn't want to do that." Now, you don't have to be a tree-killing-paper-ream-eating-user, and you can quickly stop that wasteful 1,000-page print job you didn't mean to send. The `lprm` command enables you to remove items from the printer queue. This is how you use it:

If you need to use `lprm`, follow these steps:

1. Use the `lpq` command to find the job ID number that you want to remove.

2. Invoke `lprm` with the following syntax: `lprm -P<printer name> <job ID>`.

For example, if you wanted to remove job #15 from the queue in the printer pr1, you can type

```
>lprm -Ppr1 15
```

To verify the results, you can use lpq to check the queue again:

```
>lpq -Ppr1
```

You should see the job you specified terminated and no longer active.

That's it for printing. As I have mentioned before, it is imperative that you read more about this if you really want to master printing in Unix. Unix printing is not difficult and can be learned simply by mastering the concepts brought up in this lesson, and expanding on them. Make sure you consult the Internet and man pages for more information on printing.

Summary

In this lesson, you learned the commands you need to print from the command line. The suite of lpr, lpq, and lprm commands make up the basis for printing from Unix and most Unix computers. Here's a review of some of what we covered in this lesson:

- **lpr and lp**—The lpr and lp commands are used to send a file to the printer. If the file is a type other than plain text, it can be processed by a filter that correctly formats the information for your printer.

- **lpq and lpstat**—When a print request is sent to the printer, either from lpr or enscript, it is added to the printer queue. Use the lpq or lpstat -t program to display all pending printer transactions, their corresponding job IDs, and their owners.

- **lprm and cancel**—If you want to remove a job from the print queue, lprm or cancel will do the trick.

LESSON 18

Networking and Security

In this lesson, you will learn some aspects of Unix remote access, networking, and security functionality.

In this lesson, we will cover how to remotely access your Unix system using tools such as `telnet` and `ssh` (secure shell), as well as how to use FTP (File Transfer Protocol) to send and receive files securely. You have spent so much time learning how to log in and use files, it is now time to explain to you how to do it with other Unix systems and do it securely.

Remote access is something that you might always see when working with Unix; very few and far between are the times when a Unix system is not in a protected place and locking everyone out of accessing the console directly. Because of the nature (and cost) of enterprise class hardware, Unix may only be accessed through some remote access method.

Remote access is just that—you want to access something remotely from where you are, or the system is remote from you. Regardless, it's the exact opposite of having a system on your desk where you can walk over and access the keyboard and type right into the shell prompt. Often, you will need to access this server from a local workstation (usually a Microsoft Windows system) and you connect to the Unix system with a `telnet` or secure shell. That being said, we will spend some time going over those tools and others. We will also cover the use of FTP to transfer files and how to use a web browser in KDE.

Well, you are almost at the end of the book and throughout we have touched on concepts that have helped you work with the Unix operating system to manage files, processes, and scripts.

In this chapter, we talk about how Unix is used in the networking areas of remote access and what security implications may arise from doing so.

With the proper configuration, you could spread Unix machines around the globe and at each one your user environment, files, and programs would all appear just as they do at home. This is the beauty and power of networking. Let's begin with using `telnet`.

Using `telnet`

Using `telnet` is not only very common, but also a simple to use terminal program. It is invoked by the `telnet` command on just about every operating system known to man that is running the TCP/IP protocol. TCP/IP is a protocol suite that allows `telnet` (and most of the rest of the utilities in this lesson) to function in the first place. TCP/IP is way beyond the scope of this book, but you should be familiar with what an IP address is if you are going to enter it here in the next example. As well, it should be noted that whenever you can, use `ssh`, which stands for secure shell. This protocol will provide you with encryption that can be used to secure a connection you would have normally made with the simple telnet program, which is not normally secure. Despite how insecure it is, there is still a large number of people out there that still use `telnet` all the time.

In `telnet`'s primary use, it enables you to open a login session on a remote machine. To use the `telnet` command, issue the command as follows: telnet *<remote machine>*, where *<remote machine>* is either an IP address or a hostname. You will be prompted with a login and password prompt just as if you were sitting at the console of the remote machine. From here, follow the lessons learned in Lesson 1, "Getting Started," and you will be able to log in and use your Unix system remotely.

```
> telnet 10.1.1.1
> telnet pr1
```

In the last two examples, you can see that it is easy to `telnet` to a host. You need only to add the hostname or IP address after the `telnet` command, and the system will attempt to establish a connection (and `telnet` session) with the machine you specify. Make sure you master this skill; you will be doing this frequently if you use Unix often.

IP Addressing 101   IP addressing (in its simplest definition) is a string of four numbers separated by periods
(such as 10.1.1.1) used to represent a host (computer
system) on the Internet. When a PC accesses the
Internet through an ISP, it sometimes receives a tem-
porary IP address and with that a name server assignment. This is how you surf the Internet— something
we will cover in more depth at the end of this lesson.

A hostname can only be used if you have the entry in
your hosts file (remember that file from Lesson 8,
"Text Editing," working with the vi editor) or are
working with a name server that will allow you to
specify the hostname. The server will get the IP
address back to you.

Using ssh

If you understand the concepts revolving around telnet and how to use it,
then you will have absolutely no problem understanding secure shell,
commonly referred to as ssh and invoked with the ssh command. Secure
shell is primarily used to log into another computer over a network, to
execute commands in a remote machine, and to move files from one
machine to another just as you would with telnet. The difference is, ssh
does it securely.

There are serious flaws in the telnet program as it is based on the telnet
protocol, which is part of the TCP/IP protocol suite. Without getting too
involved with what the suite is, remember that you had an IP address
before that you needed to connect to a remote system. Well, IP is a protocol and it has weaknesses because the version of it in use (version 4) has
been around just as long as Unix has. That being said, IP wasn't made for
today's script kiddie/hacker/cracker/exploiter, and does not satisfy the
need for greater security.

A newer version was created to replace the older version 4, but the newer
version is harder to implement. Also, because of the disruption it may
cause, and issues it may bring up, version 6 of the IP protocol hasn't

gained the steam it should have. So, what is the solution? This is where ssh comes in. ssh in its simplest definition is encrypted telnet. It provides strong authentication and secure communications over insecure channels, namely the Internet, or your current network, which, believe it or not, could have a sniffer on it which could capture your packets and see your unencrypted data. Although this is highly unlikely, it is completely possible. It is a replacement for telnet and rlogin and some other unsecure protocols that conform to the same cleartext model. We will cover rlogin next. Before we do, let's look at how to use ssh:

```
> ssh 10.1.1.1
> ssh pr1
```

Remember that ssh protects you only if you use it. The ssh command comes standard on most systems, but if you do not have it, ask your system administrator to set it up for you, especially if you frequently use Unix remotely.

 ssh Usage   Using the ssh command can be tricky if you have never used it. Telnet is straight forward; you enter the command and then specify the host. With ssh, it may be that easy *if* it is set up already. If not, you may get errors back. You may also need to set up encryption information on your Unix system before you use it. Just be aware of this and ask your Unix systems administrator for help if you are in a jam.

Using rlogin

The rlogin command is similar to the telnet command in that it is used for remote access and that it is not secure. However, there is one major difference: rlogin will carry some user information along with the attempt to connect.

If your account is good on several machines, they might be set up to enable you to connect between them without having to log in to each one. Try the rlogin command as follows: rlogin <remote machine>.

Variety Is the Spice of Life   Unix students ask me, "If rlogin is not good and we should only be using ssh, then why is it still supported? Why are we learning about it?" My answer is always to tell them that with everything good, there is bad, and vice versa. That's why you have variety. rlogin can also perform well. Here is an example. I have mentioned using ssh as a way to encrypt your remote access session, but that would only protect data in transit from being intercepted and read. If password sniffing, a common attack, took place, your data would be intercepted and your credentials exposed. One way to protect yourself from this exploit is to not type your password. The program rlogin can be configured to not require your password. If you know ahead of time that you'll be using your account from a given computer, you can create a file named .rhosts. You can make files and edit them, and put a line with the name of the remote computer you'll be using in that file. If you try to rlogin using the listing in the .rhosts file, you won't be asked for your password. In effect, the computer will trust the other computer for your account if you list it in your .rhosts. This is in itself a form of security, but it won't protect you from getting your credentials snatched from someone sniffing the network.

There are also some security risks associated with the use of a .rhosts file. If the remote computer gets cracked into, the attacker might see this file and realize that she can now use that account to get into other systems. This could expose the remote systems. However, if you have a good Unix administrator who knows all of these dangers and how to do a risk assessment on which ones are more important to outweigh, then your system will be safe.

An example of how to use `rlogin`:

```
> rlogin 10.1.1.1
> rlogin pr1
```

If configured properly, you will end up in a shell prompt on the remote system; if you aren't, then you will be presented with a login prompt to access the system. The `rlogin` command, because of security problems and inherent flaws in the program, is rarely used and strongly discouraged.

Using `slogin`

An alternative to `rlogin` is to use `slogin`. The `slogin` command is a remote terminal program that offers strong encryption of the data stream much like `ssh`. You are strongly encouraged to use this command if your machines don't have `ssh` installed and configured properly. Just like `rlogin`, `slogin` functions identically to `rlogin`; but it sends your login and password information, as well as anything else you type, over the network encrypted, not in clear text.

To find out whether the secure shell server is running, and to set up the `slogin` command (which needs quite a bit of configuration before you can use it), you are advised to contact your Unix system administrator. He will be more than happy to tell you about the `slogin` command or any alternatives, and to help you increase system security.

Well, up to now we have covered `telnet`, `ssh`, `rlogin`, and `slogin`. These are all remote access methods used to allow you to connect to a remote host, run commands, create scripts, and do whatever else it is you can do from the shell prompt such as transfer files from one host to another across the network.

Using `ftp`

Now that we have learned about remote access to do work at the shell prompt, what about other forms of remote work such as remote file transfer? Many times you will be called on to send or receive files much like the ones you have made, or explored within Unix already. Remember the *.rpm packages? The tar files? All of these things can be sent to other Unix systems where other people can work with them or use them if needed.

The ftp command provides you with a way to retrieve files from remote machines that aren't set up to share file systems with yours. If your machine is running an FTP server, you might be able to use it to provide your files to the rest of the world as well. Contact your system administrator about this. Remember, this book covers only the using end of Unix, so anything that needs to be added to your Unix system must be requested.

To use the ftp command, simply enter the command as follows: **ftp <ftp server>**, where the FTP server is the IP address or hostname of a remote machine running an FTP server. If you've connected properly, you'll get a prompt for your credentials, which are your username and password. It should also be noted that FTP has the same inherent problems as telnet; the information is sent in clear text.

Some FTP servers enable you to connect without an account on the system. For these, use the username *anonymous* and give your email address as the password.

Let's see how to log in with ftp:

```
> ftp 10.1.1.1
> ftp pr1
```

Once connected to an FTP site, you can cd and ls your way around. Using the command get *<filename>* enables you to retrieve a file, and put *<filename>* enables you to send one from your directory to the remote system.

Can I Secure FTP?   So, how can I secure FTP if it is also not secure? The answer is simple. You can use Secure FTP, or SFTP for short. If you have ssh installed, you will most likely have SFTP installed as it is usually part of the same client package. If you do not have it you can request it from your system administrator. Another program that you could use is also secure copy, or scp for short.

Summary

In this lesson, you were introduced to a sampling of tools that enable you to make use of the network resources around you and around the world. As you explore Unix, you'll find that this was really only a small sampling, and that there are new tools for you to use appearing constantly. Some will be replacements or upgrades for the commands outlined here, and others will be completely new. Don't be afraid to try them out. Here's a quick review of this lesson's key points:

- The `telnet` command can connect you to remote machines. If you have different accounts on different machines, you'll probably find yourself using it frequently.

- The `ssh` command can connect you to remote machines, securely. Ask your system administrator to set up `ssh` for you if you do not have it. This command should be used in lieu of `telnet` these days. It is just as easy to use, plus you get the added benefit of security.

- The `rlogin` command also connects you to remote machines, but is more useful than `telnet` if the machines you work on are configured to allow you to `rlogin` between them without giving a username or password.

- The `slogin` command provides security for remote connections. If you have it, use it. With people breaking into Unix machines daily, the network is becoming a very scary place. Using the secure connection provided by `slogin` protects your network traffic from prying eyes.

- The `ftp` command connects you with FTP servers, and enables you to transfer files around the world.

- The `sftp` command connects you with FTP servers, and enables you to securely transfer files around the world.

LESSON 19

Configuring Permissions in Unix

In this lesson, you will learn about how to configure and manage user permissions in Unix.

Wow, we have just worked through 18 lessons on how to configure Unix and we are still going strong. In the last part of this book, I will attempt to fill in some gaps in the material we just covered. For example, we talked about how the ls command when used with the -l option would provide a long listing of the files in your current directory. We briefly touched on how to read the output from the ls -l command and how it had shown the set of permissions associated with each file or directory. Now, in this lesson, we will learn more about those permissions and how to configure and manage them.

First let's discuss the importance of configuring permissions and why this is important to you, the Unix user. Unix file permissions may never be something you even work with, and they may not be something that you need to know to do your job. However, if you want to share files with other users on your system, you will need to know a little bit about the concept. Let's begin by breaking it down.

Unix File and Directory Permissions

Let's examine the output from the ls -l command. For example, type the following:

```
>ls -l

-rw-r--r-- 1 rob    rob     2024 Dec 25 20:22 39 atest.tar
-rwxrwxr-x 5 rob    rob     1024 Dec 25 20:22 atest2.tar
```

. . .

When considering file and directories, you have to understand the concept of ownership. Ownership is nothing more than noting who owns the file. Each file has information stored with it that identifies the account that owns it. From the example of ls -l, you can see that I am the owner of the two files in my current directory: atest.tar and atest2.tar. Files are owned by those who create them, although ownership can be transferred.

Each file on the Unix system also has a secondary piece of information stored that records the *group* ownership of the file.

What Is a Group?   The definition of a group is not very complex, but the application of it is. Groups are collections of users. By allowing a group to share ownership of files, many people can work together on a project and have their changes immediately available to other members of the group. Creation of groups is a system administration task, so if you need a group created for a project, talk to your system administrator.

Permissions, once applied, will control what a user (or group) can do to a file or directory. There are three basic actions, which are self-explanatory: read, write, and execute. We have already spent time covering what executables are earlier in the book. If you do not have the permissions such as read, write, or execute, then you will not be able to work with the files. It's really that simple.

- *Read* permissions control whether someone can view a file.

- *Write* allows or disallows changes to be made to a file.

- *Execute* permissions control whether a file can be run, or executed.

Directory Permissions Specifics

We just covered files, but what about the directories that hold the files? Permission rights for directories are slightly different than those of files. If a directory has execute permissions turned off, you cannot change into that directory (using the cd command), view its contents, or write to it. It is effectively turned off. If read permissions are turned off, you can still create files in the directory and read them, but you cannot get a listing of what is in the directory. Lastly, if the write permission for a directory is turned off, you can view a listing of the contents and read files, but you cannot create any new files.

Permission Levels

When permissions are applied to a file or directory, they are applied at three specific levels: owner, group, and world.

- The *user* (sometimes called *owner*) permissions simply control what permissions the file owner has.

- *Group* permissions determine what actions can be performed by members of the same group to which the file belongs. Your system administrator can create new groups, or add you as a member of a group.

- *Other* (sometimes called *world*) permissions are for a huge group that encompasses all the users on your computer. For example, email-related directories often assume other permissions.

If there is guest access to your computer, you can assume that any active other permissions apply to anyone who can access your computer.

Using ls -l

In this book, we have already spent a large amount of time using the ls command so our coverage here will be at a minimum. In this example, we will use the -l option. If you run ls -l to list your directories, you can see the owner, group, and associated permissions for any file. Some versions of ls won't show you the owner and group simultaneously with this command. Usually, they list group and owner if you add the -g option, as in ls -lg.

For an example of using ls -l, type the following:

```
>ls -l

-rw-r--r-- 1 rob   rob      2024 Dec 25 20:00 atest.tar
drwxrwxr-x 5 rob   rob      1024 Dec 25 20:22 test

...
```

The information that we are most concerned with dissecting is the first, third, and fourth columns. The first column identifies the owner, group, and other permissions that are active for a file or directory. The first character is a *d* if the file type is a directory. In this example, I have a test directory I created with the mkdir command. Normally this is a - for a normal file, which you can see for my atest.tar file. The remainder of the characters, as you might guess, stand for *read (r)*, *write (w)*, and *execute (x)*. The first three characters (following the initial - or *d* character) are the active owner permissions, the second three characters are the group permissions, and the last three are other permissions. It is important to memorize these settings, because this is how you know how secure your file or directory is. This tells you what the world can do to your files, such as change or delete them if the permissions are too generous. Moving on, we see the third column is the file owner, me. The fourth column is the group owner, which is again me. The rest of the information is simply the size of the file, the date of creation, the time, and the name of the file or directory.

Using chmod

Now that you know what permissions are, you probably want to know how to change them, because listing them can only get you so far. Listing them will help you to get a good grip on what is there, but to make changes you need to take the next step, which is to use the chmod command. There are two modes of operation that you can use with chmod: a quick-and-dirty mode, and a more user-friendly way of setting permissions.

The user-friendly mode uses easy-to-remember commands to set or unset permissions. To use this, do the following:

1. Pick a *permission level*. If you want to set permissions for the owner, the level is **u**. If you want to change permissions for the group, it is **g**. For other permissions, choose **o**. Lastly, if you want to affect all the levels of permissions (owner, group, and other), use **a**.

2. Choose an *operation*. Decide whether you want to set (turn on) or unset (turn off) a particular level of permission. If you want to set a permission, the operation is **+**; if you want to unset a permission, it is **-**.

3. Choose the *permission* itself. If you want to operate on the read permission, choose **r**, for write choose **w**, and for execute choose **x**.

4. Issue the chmod command in this manner: chmod `<permission level><operation><permission>` `<filename>` `<filename>` `. . . .`

Let's look at an example of chmod in action. It is important that you pay close attention to this lesson and try to walk away with this knowledge if you are moving from end user to system administrator. Not knowing how to set permissions will almost always ruin your chances for advancement because you will not be able to do anything without knowing how to change permissions.

The chmod command sets Unix file permissions exactly how you want them, so let's take a look at how. First you need to be connected to your Unix system. Because you will not always be on a local system, you may need to connect to a remote system, log in, change some permissions, and then exit the session using telnet or ssh. Once in the shell prompt, you need to execute a chmod command. Here are some examples of what you can do with the chmod command:

```
> chmod 0755 script.sh
> chmod 755 script.sh
> chmod u=rwx,g=rx,o=rx script.sh
```

Let's look at a real example. To activate group write permissions for the script.sh file shown here, type the following:

```
-rw------- 1 rob   test 1662882 Dec  25 12:00 script.sh
>chmod g+w script.sh
```

To see if this worked, you can run ls -l on the filename as follows:

```
>ls -l script.sh

-rw--w---- 1 rob   test 1662882 Dec  25 12:00 script.sh
```

Write permissions have been activated for the test group members. Because of its symbolic nature, this method for adjusting file permissions might be easy for some; however, there is another syntax that you might find more efficient and effective. In this example, you can set the actual bit mask that is used to control a file's permissions. The bit mask would be the three binary bits used to represent each level of permission. The three binary bits would be (in order from left to right):

- 1st bit: (start from the left) controls read

- 2nd bit: controls write

- 3rd bit: controls execute

There, those are your three permissions, and now you can view our example here as binary numbers translated to decimal:

```
100 - Read permission - The decimal equivalent of this binary
value is 4.
```

```
010 - Write permission - The decimal value for write is 2.
001 - Execute permission - The decimal representation is 1.
```

So this is the layout, and you would need to understand the concepts of Boolean math a bit, but if you don't, Table 19.1 will serve you well:

TABLE 19.1 Permission Bits

3rd Bit Read	2nd Bit Write	1st Bit Execute
100	010	001
4	2	1

To figure this out you need to know how binary numbers are converted to decimal. You need only to know how to convert the first three numbers. From moving from right to left, start to count from 1 and move up by the power of 2 each time, so you would have 1, 2, and then 4, correct? If that is the case, then you need to know that if you took the first bunch of three 001 and counted from left to right saying that 0 is "off" and a 1 is "on," the first one count from right to left by 1, 2, and 4 would be 1. Now take the next example—010. This one is two because the middle column in our example of 1, 2, 4 from the right to left would mean that 0 is off (so no 1), then 2 is on, then 4 is off. Get it now? How about the last one... 100.

With this example, you can quickly figure out the decimal number you need to use; instead of setting permissions the other way, you can specify them as such.

Using this technique, you can easily set multiple permissions simultaneously. For example, it's easy to see that 110 is the combination of the read and write permissions. The decimal value of this binary string is 6 (4+2). I now have my setting for read and write permissions. To use this method of setting a file's permissions, you set permissions for owner, group, and other simultaneously. Each of these digits is the sum of the permissions that you want to set. The first digit is the owner, the second is the group, and the third is other.

For example, suppose that you want to set the owner to have full permissions, and the group and other to have read and execute permissions. Full permissions are achieved by adding all the permission values (4+2+1=7). Read and execute permissions are a combination of 4+1=5. The three numbers you'll use to set this are 7, 5, and 5, entered as a single three-digit number, 755. The syntax for this form of chmod is as follows:

chmod <permissions> <filename> <filename> ....

For example, check out the following:

```
>chmod 755 script.sh
>ls -lg script.sh

-rwxr-xr-x 1 rob   test 1663882 Dec 25 script.sh
```

As you might hope, the owner has full read, write, and execute permissions, whereas the group and other have read and execute permissions. As you become experienced, you'll probably find that this second method is the fastest way to set permissions. Just remember read (4), write (2), and execute (1), and you'll be fine.

Changing Permissions Recursively   If you want to change the permissions of all the files and directories within any directory, you can use the -R option with the chmod command to recursively change everything within a directory.

This example performs recursive chmod for the directory:

```
> chmod -R 755 somedirectory
```

You should feel comfortable with changing permissions if you understood everything completely, and no fear if you didn't. This is why I harp on practice so much, to make sure that you will keep doing this until you can read permissions and their placement every time you run the ls -l command.

Now that you are familiar with all these difficult concepts, let's build on them to show you how to change a group setting.

Using `chgrp`

Although you can't change a file's owner, you can change the group that a file belongs to. You can do this with the `chgrp` command. `chgrp` is a Unix command used to change the group setting. The `chgrp` command stands for "change group." The `chgrp` command marks a file as being part of a different group. To do this, however, you must be a member of that group. Your Unix system administrator has the capability to create new groups and add users to these groups. If you have any questions about your own group membership(s), ask your administrator how your account was configured.

To use `chgrp`, follow these steps:

1. Choose the file or files you want to change.

2. Determine which group the file now belongs to.

3. Change the file's group using the following command: `chgrp`
   <new group> <filename> <filename> ....

For example, type the following:

```
>chgrp admins script.sh
>ls -lg script.sh

-rwxr-xr-x 1 rob admins 1463882 Dec 25 12:00
(output removed)
```

The `script.sh` file now belongs to the group admins. Members of the group have read and execute permissions for the file. The most obvious use for `chgrp` is if you are collaborating on a project. If you create a file that you want to share with many people, you'll need to change the group of the file to one that all the users belong to.

Be Careful with What You Change   Be careful when setting permissions. If you change something too drastically, you can really get into trouble. Changing permissions can also lock you out of something, so be careful using this lesson in a production environment if you are just learning Unix. Consider what can happen, for the worse.

Summary

One more lesson to go! You have come a long way from just logging into Unix to now setting permissions on files and directories. You should be very proud to be a Unix user with some solid skills learned entirely from scratch. In our next lesson, we will wrap up the book with a few more high-end commands that you can experiment with and incorporate into your other lessons, such as scripting, for example.

In this lesson, you learned the purpose of permissions, owners, and groups, which is very important to know if you want to do more than just list data in a directory. Now you can read that list and understand who has access to what and how to set that access if needed. You now know how to do this not only by setting permissions as we did, but also changing the group on the file or directory as well. You now understand what is necessary to enable other users to access your files and how to collaborate on projects using group permissions. You might want to take a few minutes to talk to your system administrator to find out how she has decided to manage groups. Also, you might want to request that groups be created that include other users with whom you want to share files.

Following is a look at some of the highlights from this lesson:

- **Permissions**—File permissions control who can access a file, and what level of access they have to a file. The three levels of permissions are read, write, and execute. These permissions can be applied to the owner, group, or other.

- **chmod**—The chmod command changes the permissions for a file or directory. There are two methods of operation: symbolic and numeric. They both accomplish the same thing, so use the one you feel comfortable with.

- **chgrp**—You can change the group that a file belongs to with the chgrp function. You can change only the file to a group that you belong to.

LESSON 20

Unix Privileged Commands

In this lesson, you'll take a look at some of the restricted commands that Unix system administrators use, and learn some of the other things you can do with your Unix system.

In this chapter we celebrate you not only reaching the end of the book (congratulations!) but to also welcome you to the "power-user" ranks. If you have successfully navigated through this book and have been practicing so that you can recall all the commands and some of their options that we learned about, then you are ready for the next step.

The commands in this section are restricted commands that are mostly used by Unix system administrators. It doesn't hurt to know about them and how they work so that if you are interested, you can dig deeper into them and start on the path to being a Unix system administrator. If not, knowing these commands surely puts you at the advantage because knowledge is power. Just fill your brain with as much Unix as you can, and before long you will be typing commands quickly and know exactly what it is you are doing.

In this lesson, I open the doors to a few new concepts and hope that after this lesson is done, you are efficiently typing the learned commands and their proper options in the shell prompt with no problems.

For those who may have forgotten about root, let's quickly discuss it.

Root Refresher

In this lesson, we discuss commands that are used only as root. So we are all on the same page here, let's go back over what root is. It is critically important you know root and it does have two different meanings.

You Need to Be Root   In this lesson, you'll take a look at some of the restricted commands that Unix system administrators use, and learn some of the other things you can do with your Unix system. The commands in this lesson are restricted to being run by the root user, but the information here will help you understand some of root's concerns and help conversations with your system administrator to make a little more sense. Because of the way that Unix works (with multiple users, multiple processes, and files owned by potentially hundreds of people), there are certain commands that will cause chaos if entrusted to normal users. These commands do things such as format disks, reboot the system, and create or remove devices.

Root technically has two definitions in Unix. For one, it's the name of the login account given full and complete access to all system resources.

The root directory is another one, which is also used to describe the directory named /. This is the top-level drive to where all the rest of the Unix system branches off from.

Make sure you are logged in as the root (user account) so that you can work with any of the commands seen here. If you cannot log in as root at work, follow along and wait until you can set up a test lab at home so you can work on these root-level commands. Making mistakes with these commands is even more unforgiving then any other command we have learned so far. These could really cause serious issues to the system if not done correctly. You need to make sure you practice before doing these commands in a live setting.

Using the su Command The su command creates a shell with the user ID of another user.

sudo (pronounced soo-doo) simply stands for "SuperUser do." sudo is used to allow any user to run some, if not all, root-level commands using that account. Make sure you consider this and make it just as important as the root account, because it's easy to see how quickly it can be exploited.

Single-User Mode

Single-user mode is a Unix system mode from bootup created for administrative and maintenance activities, a mode where the machine has no network resources and can only support a single user logged in. Single-user mode will absolutely demand complete control of the system. When the system is in this single-user mode, whoever is logged in becomes root. This is, however, a minimal system startup state so don't fear, it is merely for diagnostics. If you do become interested in repairing a non-booting Unix system, or want to try to repair problems in your system, you may want to learn about this mode. Only the root partition is mounted, so only commands that reside in the root file system are available. As well, every Unix machine can be configured to boot into *single-user mode*.

Single-user mode can also be viewed as a maintenance mode that enables the root user to repair problems with the system without having to worry about other users changing things that they are working on. This is essentially what it is used for. If you have bootup problems, then ask your system administrator, and look yourself to see what is done.

With some versions of Unix, if a machine experiences a particularly hard crash, it might reboot itself into single-user mode automatically. This is why you may see it as a Unix end user; if you notice something different, then ask for help. The system may have suffered a hard crash and is now waiting for your help!

Some versions of Unix and Linux will require you to give up a root password before any commands can be entered, and others come up directly into a root shell; this varies by distribution and configuration. If you happen to crash a Unix machine and it comes up in single-user mode, it is better you do absolutely nothing and ask for help because the system is prepped for the experienced administrator, not the inexperienced end user. If the wrong things are entered, the system could become worse, or logging and troubleshooting data can be lost. Anything you do has the potential to make diagnosing the crash impossible; worse, it can have devastating effects on the system. At the same time, if you are at home in your lab, go to town. Look online or get more books on how to figure out how to operate this mode and try to simulate issues to get yourself comfortable with troubleshooting and entering the mode manually.

fsck

The fsck command (short for "file system check" or "file system consistency check") will start the Unix system utility to check the consistency of your file system. Every now and again you might hear a Unix system administrator talking about the need to fsck a hard drive because it is experiencing problems. Hard disks are like light bulbs: They are made to fail and actually have a MTBF (Mean Time Between Failure) associated with them. This just means that like a light bulb, their internal parts will eventually quit and cease to function due to nonstop use and/or damage.

The fsck command is Unix's disk fixer program, and it is used to clean up problems caused by crashes or errant pieces of software. Much like the tools used in Microsoft Windows systems (such as ScanDisk and defrag), you will eventually need to know this command if you are managing and maintaining a Unix system. Most Unix systems fsck their drives on bootup, and the expected result is an analysis report containing the number of files and the fragmentation level of the drive. If you're watching a Unix machine boot, do not be overly concerned if you see fsck report problems. Unix automatically attempts to fix them.

In most cases, fsck will be successful at the repair and fix. After using fsck on the drives, the system restarts the reboot process, which should then bring you to the login prompt. If the drives have serious problems, the automatic fsck exits with the following error message: Run fsck by hand.

Here is what the whole message would look like on some distros of Unix or Linux.

```
checking root filesystems parallelizing fsck version 1.04 [/
➡sbin/fsck.ext2] fsck.ext2 -a /dev/sda1 /dev/sda1
➡ contains a file system with errors check forced
➡ Block 23454345665 of inode 143234 > Blocks
➡(10234234) /dev/sda1: UNEXPECTED INCONSISTENCY; Run
➡ fsck manually an error occurred during the file
➡system check. Dropping you to a shell; the system
➡will reboot when you leave the shell
```

If it does, please don't touch anything, and go find a system administrator for help. If you are running this in your lab, then this is also tied to what we just learned; you may be booting in single-user mode and need to run fsck. If you have a crash after booting, you should run fsck from a boot disk, which may be the same ones you used to install Unix or Linux in your lab. In this example, you can run fsck /dev/sda1 (the partition that is showing the errors) and fsck will attempt the fix. fsck will prompt you to find and fix each error so you can see what it is. Again, this is only something you should do in a lab, or as an experienced user.

shutdown/reboot

There may be a time where you need to shut down your Unix system or reboot it. Although I can vouch from many years of experience that you will reboot Unix or Linux far less than Microsoft Windows, you may still need to shut down your system or reboot it. Unix boots differently than Microsoft Windows. Most Windows operating systems will boot up as a complete unit. In Unix, the kernel loads, and then anything else is loaded around it for use. Unix uses dozens of programs to form what appears to be a huge operating system, when in reality it's all loaded separately as single programs.

Each of these programs might be in the process of modifying, moving, creating, or deleting files at any point in time and cannot be interrupted. If you simply shut off the power to a Unix machine, you interrupt all these processes, and probably destroy any files they were working on at the time. This happens often, and is another reason why it's important that commands like this are restricted to the proper users. Haphazardly shutting off the power to a Unix machine has the potential to completely corrupt the drives, leaving the system unusable. Be careful if you use this command at work. If you are working in your lab, then have fun, and try to create problems so that you can use single-user mode and fsck to fix it.

The shutdown command and a reboot command have obvious goals. These two commands gracefully exit all running software, write out disk-cache information to the drives, and complete their respective tasks. They are restricted to the root user for obvious reasons.

Summary

In this lesson, you were introduced to root level commands that if not used properly could cause serious problems. However, if these commands are mastered and practiced, they can help you in a great many ways that this 10-minute lesson could never cover in this page count. Make sure that if any of these commands interest you, and you want to progress on further past this book, set up a Unix or Linux system at home or in a lab somewhere and practice! It is truly the only way to really get good at this, especially something as cryptic as Unix. You need to practice and read more.

To tie up the book, I would personally like to wish you the best in your Unix studies beyond this point. I hope you enjoyed this book and that you learned enough to get to the next level. Let me know at rshimonski@rsnetworks.net or visit me on the web at http://www. rsnetworks.net. It truly has been a pleasure to teach you the fundamentals of Unix. The following is a review of some of the other points from this lesson:

- Never touch a machine if it looks like it's running a root shell. Root is powerful and should only be used by experienced users and system administrators.

- Never ever turn the power to your machine off without permission from your administrator. If you've got a shutdown button on your machine, pretend it doesn't even exist.

- Root (administrative users) can change ownership of files for you, but consider whether it's really necessary or whether a copy will do.

APPENDIX A

Learn More About Unix: Reference

Now that you are familiar with the operation of Unix, you can continue to learn more by visiting online resources. The Internet is an excellent resource to find information on Unix and Linux. I hope that this list is a gateway into the endless sea of what is out there. Make sure you continue your studies with Unix and practice as much as possible. Remember, the more you practice, the easier it gets. As soon as you know the commands cold, your control of Unix strengthens. I have also included some websites of Unix and Linux vendors; most have helpful tutorials and online documentation. These websites offer valuable information for specific operating systems. For example, if you were running Sun Solaris and needed to know Unix-based commands that may be specific to that operating system, you would want to visit the Sun website (http://www.sun.com). I also provided a few links to Linux vendors who sell inexpensive desktop operating systems that are full-blown versions of Linux. Linux is similar to Unix, so if you can manage Linux, install it and practice as much as you can; your mastery of Unix will come quickly. In addition to reading a book like this, you can find more information on the following websites:

Unix Reference:

http://www.freebsd.org/
http://www.ugu.com/
http://www.unix.org/
http://www.sco.com/
http://www.unixreview.com/

Linux Reference:

http://www.tldp.org/
http://slashdot.org
http://www.linux.com/
http://www.linuxjournal.com/
http://www.linuxquestions.org/
http://www.novell.com/linux/
http://www.redhat.com/
http://www.google.com/linux

General Reference:

http://www.rsnetworks.net/masterunixquickly/
http://www.gnu.org/
http://blackboxwm.sourceforge.net/

INDEX